Bourne Klein

BLEACH

REBIRTH OF SOULS

GAME GUIDE

Unleash your Bankai by mastering every battle to dominate every fight.

CHAPTER 1: INTRODUCTION TO BLEACH REBIRTH OF SOULS

1.1 OVERVIEW OF THE GAME

BLEACH: Rebirth of Souls is an action-packed 3D fighting game that brings the legendary *Bleach* anime and manga series to life. Developed by Tamsoft Corporation and published by Bandai Namco Entertainment, the game is designed to deliver high-energy combat, deep character customization, and a thrilling experience for fans and newcomers alike.

Set in the *Bleach* universe, the game allows players to step into the shoes of powerful warriors, including Ichigo Kurosaki, Rukia Kuchiki, Byakuya Kuchiki, Kenpachi Zaraki, and many more. Each character wields their iconic Zanpakutō, unleashing devastating Shikai and Bankai transformations to dominate battles.

The game features multiple modes, including Story Mode, Versus Battles, and Online PvP, offering a mix of solo and competitive gameplay. Whether you're reliving Ichigo's journey from a substitute Soul Reaper to a legendary warrior or testing your skills against real players worldwide, *BLEACH: Rebirth of Souls* delivers intense action and strategic depth.

This guide is designed to be your ultimate companion, helping you master the game, refine your combat techniques, unlock hidden secrets, and rise through the ranks to become an elite fighter.

1.2 STORYLINE AND SETTING

BLEACH: Rebirth of Souls immerses players in the vast and dynamic world of *Bleach*, faithfully recreating the high-stakes battles and emotional depth that made the series a global phenomenon. The game follows the journey of Ichigo Kurosaki, a high school student who unexpectedly inherits the powers of a Soul Reaper, a warrior tasked with protecting the living world from malevolent spirits known as Hollows.

As Ichigo steps into this dangerous role, he becomes entangled in an epic struggle involving powerful enemies, ancient rivalries, and hidden conspiracies that threaten the balance between the Human World, Soul Society, and Hueco Mundo. The game's Story Mode takes players through some of the most defining arcs of *Bleach*, from Ichigo's initial awakening to his climactic battles against formidable foes like Sōsuke Aizen, Grimmjow Jaegerjaquez, and Ulquiorra Cifer.

The settings are as iconic as the characters themselves, ranging from the peaceful town of Karakura, where Ichigo's journey begins, to the Soul Society, home of the Soul Reapers, and the desolate wastelands of Hueco Mundo, the domain of the Arrancars. Each environment is meticulously crafted to reflect its source material, bringing familiar locations to life with stunning visuals and dynamic battle arenas.

Beyond the main story, *Rebirth of Souls* introduces Secret Story mode, where players can explore untold moments, alternate scenarios, and deep character backstories. This mode expands on what fans know from the anime and manga, offering what-if battles and character interactions that provide fresh perspectives on the *Bleach* universe.

Whether you're reliving your favorite moments or discovering new twists in the story, *BLEACH: Rebirth of Souls* ensures an unforgettable experience, blending faithful storytelling, immersive settings, and exhilarating combat into a single epic adventure.

1.3 KEY FEATURES AND GAME MODES

BLEACH: Rebirth of Souls isn't just another anime fighting game—it's a high-intensity, strategy-driven battle experience that combines fluid combat, cinematic transformations, and deep character customization. Designed to appeal to both casual players and competitive fighters, the game offers a rich selection of modes and features to keep the action fresh and engaging.

KEY FEATURES

Dynamic Combat System – The game uses a unique momentum-based battle system where precise timing, well-placed counters, and smart use of abilities can turn the tide of battle. Every clash feels impactful, rewarding players who master their character's strengths.

Authentic Bleach Character Roster – Play as fan-favorite heroes and villains, each with unique Zanpakutō abilities, Shikai transformations, and Bankai power-ups. From Ichigo's devastating Getsuga Tenshō to Byakuya's elegant yet deadly Senbonzakura Kageyoshi, every character feels true to their manga and anime origins.

Iconic Locations – Fight across beautifully rendered stages inspired by the *Bleach* universe, including Karakura Town, Soul Society, Hueco Mundo, and Wandenreich. Each stage comes with its own environmental hazards and destructible elements, making battles even more intense.

Unlockable Content and Secret Battles – Players can unlock hidden characters, alternative costumes, and special battle scenarios by completing in-game challenges, rewarding exploration and mastery.

 Explosive Special Moves and Cinematic Finishes – Execute powerful finishing moves with stunning anime-inspired cutscenes, making every victory feel like a moment straight out of the show.

GAME MODES

Story Mode – Relive the legendary arcs of *Bleach*, from Ichigo's first encounter with Soul Reapers to the Thousand-Year Blood War. Featuring fully voiced cutscenes and dramatic in-game battles, this mode lets players experience the anime's most iconic fights firsthand.

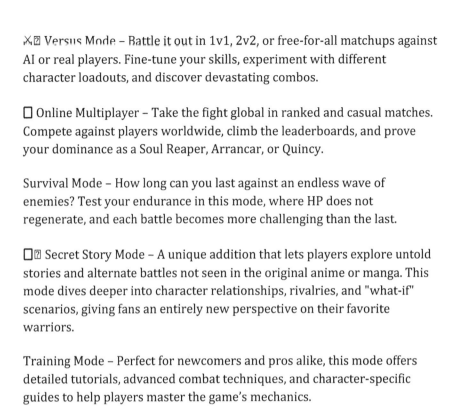

⚔️ Versus Mode – Battle it out in 1v1, 2v2, or free-for-all matchups against AI or real players. Fine-tune your skills, experiment with different character loadouts, and discover devastating combos.

☐ Online Multiplayer – Take the fight global in ranked and casual matches. Compete against players worldwide, climb the leaderboards, and prove your dominance as a Soul Reaper, Arrancar, or Quincy.

Survival Mode – How long can you last against an endless wave of enemies? Test your endurance in this mode, where HP does not regenerate, and each battle becomes more challenging than the last.

☐⚡ Secret Story Mode – A unique addition that lets players explore untold stories and alternate battles not seen in the original anime or manga. This mode dives deeper into character relationships, rivalries, and "what-if" scenarios, giving fans an entirely new perspective on their favorite warriors.

Training Mode – Perfect for newcomers and pros alike, this mode offers detailed tutorials, advanced combat techniques, and character-specific guides to help players master the game's mechanics.

BLEACH: Rebirth of Souls isn't just about fighting—it's about strategy, skill, and immersing yourself in the world of Soul Reapers and Arrancars. Whether you're here for the story, the competitive battles, or just to pull off that perfect Bankai finish, there's a mode for every type of player.

Get ready to step into the battlefield—because in this world, only the strongest survive.

1.4 WHAT TO EXPECT IN THIS GUIDE

Whether you're a first-time player stepping into the world of *BLEACH: Rebirth of Souls* or a seasoned fighter looking to refine your skills, this guide is designed to be your ultimate companion. Packed with expert strategies, in-depth character analysis, and step-by-step walkthroughs, this book will help you master every aspect of the game—from the fundamentals to advanced techniques that separate casual players from top-tier competitors.

A COMPLETE BREAKDOWN OF GAMEPLAY MECHANICS

Understanding the core mechanics of *Rebirth of Souls* is crucial for success. This guide will break down:

- The combat system, including light, heavy, and spiritual attacks

- How to execute powerful combos and chain attacks effectively

- The importance of blocking, dodging, and countering to gain an edge in battle

- How to unleash Shikai and Bankai transformations at the right moment

By the time you finish reading, you'll know how to control the battlefield like a true Soul Reaper.

DETAILED CHARACTER CLASS AND PLAYSTYLE ANALYSIS

Not all fighters are the same! Whether you prefer brute-force melee combat, swift tactical strikes, or long-range energy attacks, this guide will help you choose a character that fits your unique playstyle. Inside, you'll find:

- A full character roster breakdown, including each fighter's strengths, weaknesses, and best matchups

- Tips on choosing the right character for different modes (Story, PvP, Survival)

- Hidden mechanics that separate good players from great players

MASTERING GAME MODES AND UNLOCKING SECRETS

From Story Mode to Online Battles, this guide provides detailed strategies for every major game mode, ensuring you:

- Dominate Story Mode by understanding enemy attack patterns and weaknesses

- Climb the online leaderboards with high-level PvP strategies

- Survive endless waves in Survival Mode with expert stamina management

- Unlock secret characters, hidden fights, and rare collectibles

ACHIEVING 100% COMPLETION

If you're a completionist, this guide will help you check every achievement and trophy off your list. Learn how to:

- Complete difficult challenges for exclusive in-game rewards

- Unlock hidden endings and alternative battle outcomes

- Master time-sensitive missions and special event content

FOR CASUAL PLAYERS AND HARDCORE COMPETITORS ALIKE

This isn't just a button-mashing game—it's a technical fighter that rewards precision, patience, and strategy. Whether you're here for the story, the challenge, or the competition, this guide will give you the knowledge, skills, and insider secrets to play at your best.

So gear up, awaken your Bankai, and get ready to become the Ultimate Warrior in BLEACH: Rebirth of Souls!

CHAPTER 2: SYSTEM REQUIREMENTS AND INSTALLATION

2.1 MINIMUM AND RECOMMENDED SYSTEM REQUIREMENTS

Before diving into the high-intensity battles of *BLEACH: Rebirth of Souls*, it's essential to ensure your system meets the game's technical requirements. Whether you're playing on PC or console, meeting or exceeding these specs guarantees smooth performance, crisp visuals, and lag-free combat.

Below, you'll find the official system requirements for the PC version, along with key details for console players.

MINIMUM SYSTEM REQUIREMENTS (PC)

To run the game at a playable level with decent visuals and stable performance, your PC must meet at least these specifications:

- OS: Windows 10 (64-bit)

- Processor: Intel Core i5-8400 / AMD Ryzen 3 3300X

- Memory: 8 GB RAM

- Graphics: NVIDIA GeForce GTX 1060 (6GB) / AMD Radeon RX 580

- DirectX: Version 12

- Storage: 50 GB available space

- Internet: Broadband connection required for online features

At this level, expect 1080p resolution at 30-60 FPS, though you may need to adjust settings for smoother gameplay.

RECOMMENDED SYSTEM REQUIREMENTS (PC)

For optimal performance with higher resolution, faster load times, and fluid combat, aim for these specs:

- OS: Windows 11 (64-bit)

- Processor: Intel Core i7-9700K / AMD Ryzen 5 5600X

- Memory: 16 GB RAM

- Graphics: NVIDIA GeForce RTX 3060 / AMD Radeon RX 6700 XT

- DirectX: Version 12

- Storage: 50 GB SSD (solid-state drive recommended for faster loading)

- Internet: High-speed connection for online battles

With these specs, expect 1440p or even 4K resolution, stable 60+ FPS, and maxed-out visual settings without performance drops.

CONSOLE PERFORMANCE (PS5, XBOX SERIES X/S, PS4, XBOX ONE)

While console players don't have to worry about system specs, performance varies depending on the hardware:

- PlayStation 5 & Xbox Series X/S – Supports 4K resolution, 60 FPS gameplay, and faster loading times.

- PlayStation 4 & Xbox One – Runs at 1080p, 30-60 FPS, with some visual compromises on older models.

To get the best experience, playing on next-gen consoles or a high-end PC is highly recommended.

ADDITIONAL REQUIREMENTS AND CONSIDERATIONS

Online Play Requirements – An internet connection is required for multiplayer and online features. Console players may need PlayStation Plus or Xbox Game Pass Ultimate for online battles.

Controller Support – The PC version is fully compatible with gamepads, and using a controller is highly recommended for smoother combat execution.

VRR & Performance Modes – On next-gen consoles, players can choose between performance mode (higher FPS) and quality mode (higher resolution), ensuring a tailored experience based on preference.

FINAL VERDICT: IS YOUR SYSTEM READY?

If your PC meets the minimum requirements, you'll be able to enjoy *BLEACH: Rebirth of Souls*—but if you want the full experience with fluid animations, faster response times, and breathtaking visuals, aiming for the recommended specs or playing on next-gen consoles is the way to go.

Prepare your system, power up, and get ready for battle!

2.2 INSTALLATION GUIDE FOR PC AND CONSOLES

Getting *BLEACH: Rebirth of Souls* up and running is a straightforward process, but ensuring a smooth installation requires following the right steps based on your platform. Whether you're playing on PC, PlayStation, or Xbox, this guide will walk you through everything—from downloading the game to optimizing settings for the best experience.

INSTALLING ON PC (STEAM OR OTHER PLATFORMS)

STEP 1: CHECK YOUR SYSTEM REQUIREMENTS

Before installing, double-check that your PC meets the minimum or recommended system requirements (refer to section 2.1).

STEP 2: PURCHASE AND DOWNLOAD THE GAME

- Steam Version

  - Open the Steam client (or download it from store.steampowered.com if you don't have it).

  - Log in to your Steam account or create one if needed.

  - In the Steam Store, search for *BLEACH: Rebirth of Souls* and purchase it.

  - Click Install to begin downloading the game.

- Other PC Platforms (Epic Games, Microsoft Store, etc.)

- The process is similar: search, purchase, and download through the respective launcher.

STEP 3: INSTALL AND CONFIGURE SETTINGS

- Once downloaded, Steam (or your platform) will handle the automatic installation.

- When installation is complete, launch the game and head to Settings to adjust graphics, resolution, and keybindings for your setup.

STEP 4: UPDATE DRIVERS AND OPTIMIZE PERFORMANCE

For the best performance:
Update your GPU drivers (NVIDIA, AMD, or Intel).
Close background applications to free up RAM and CPU resources.
Adjust in-game graphics settings if needed for a smooth frame rate.

INSTALLING ON PLAYSTATION (PS4 & PS5)

STEP 1: PURCHASE AND DOWNLOAD THE GAME

- Open the PlayStation Store from your PS4 or PS5 dashboard.

- Search for *BLEACH: Rebirth of Souls* and complete your purchase.

- After purchasing, select Download to begin the installation.

STEP 2: INSTALLING FROM A PHYSICAL DISC (IF AVAILABLE)

- Insert the game disc into your PS4 or PS5.

- The installation process will begin automatically.

- If prompted, download any updates or patches before launching.

STEP 3: OPTIMIZE GAME SETTINGS

- On PS5, you can switch between Performance Mode (higher FPS) and Resolution Mode (higher visuals) in the system settings.

- On PS4, check for game updates to ensure optimal stability.

INSTALLING ON XBOX (XBOX ONE & XBOX SERIES X/S)

STEP 1: DOWNLOADING THE DIGITAL VERSION

- Open the Microsoft Store from your Xbox dashboard.

- Search for *BLEACH: Rebirth of Souls* and purchase the game.

- Select Install and wait for the download to complete.

STEP 2: INSTALLING FROM A DISC (IF AVAILABLE)

- Insert the game disc into your Xbox One or Xbox Series X.

- The game will install automatically. If an update is required, allow it to download before playing.

STEP 3: ADJUSTING PERFORMANCE SETTINGS

- On Xbox Series X/S, go to Settings → General → TV & Display Options and choose 120Hz mode for smoother gameplay if your display supports it.

- On Xbox One, make sure storage space is available to prevent installation errors.

POST-INSTALLATION TIPS FOR ALL PLATFORMS

Enable Auto-Updates – Keeping the game updated ensures you have the latest patches, bug fixes, and balance updates.

Check for DLC and Bonus Content – If you pre-ordered or purchased a special edition, redeem any extra characters, costumes, or in-game bonuses.

Link Online Accounts (Optional) – If the game supports cross-save or cloud storage, linking your account can help save progress across multiple platforms.

FINAL STEP: JUMP INTO THE ACTION!

Once installation is complete, fire up the game, tweak your settings, and dive into the world of BLEACH!

Your journey as a Soul Reaper begins now—get ready to battle!

2.3 FIRST-TIME SETUP AND CONFIGURATION

So, you've successfully installed *BLEACH: Rebirth of Souls*—welcome to the battlefield! But before you jump into action, proper setup and configuration can make all the difference in your gameplay experience. From adjusting controls and graphics to setting up online preferences, this guide ensures that your first steps into the game are smooth, optimized, and battle-ready.

STEP 1: ADJUSTING DISPLAY AND GRAPHICS SETTINGS *(FOR PC & NEXT-GEN CONSOLES)*

To fully immerse yourself in the world of *BLEACH*, you'll want crisp visuals and smooth frame rates. Here's how to set up your display for the best experience:

PC PLAYERS (GRAPHICS OPTIMIZATION)

1. Go to Settings → Graphics

2. Adjust the following based on your PC's performance:

   - Resolution: Set to native (1080p, 1440p, or 4K) for clear visuals.

   - Frame Rate: Choose 60 FPS or higher for fluid combat.

   - Shadow & Texture Quality: Medium to High (Lower if experiencing lag).

   - Anti-Aliasing: Adjust to reduce jagged edges.

   - V-Sync: Enable if you experience screen tearing.

   - Ray Tracing (If Available): Turn on for enhanced lighting (but note it affects performance).

3. Click Apply Changes and test your settings in a practice match.

CONSOLE PLAYERS (PERFORMANCE VS. RESOLUTION MODE)

- On PS5 & Xbox Series X, go to:
  Settings → Graphics Mode and choose:

    - Performance Mode (Higher FPS, Lower Visual Detail) – Best for competitive battles.

    - Resolution Mode (Higher Visuals, Lower FPS) – Best for cinematic story mode experience.

- On PS4 & Xbox One, ensure motion blur and unnecessary effects are turned off for a smoother experience.

STEP 2: CUSTOMIZING CONTROLS & KEYBINDINGS

CONTROLLER SETUP (RECOMMENDED FOR CONSOLE & PC PLAYERS)

BLEACH: Rebirth of Souls is designed to be fast-paced, so having the right control setup is key. If the default layout doesn't suit your playstyle, customize it:

1. Go to Settings → Controls

2. Adjust button mappings for:

    - Light Attacks, Heavy Attacks, and Special Moves

    - Dodge, Block, and Counter Buttons

    - Triggering Bankai or Ultimate Abilities

3. If using a PlayStation DualSense or Xbox Controller on PC, enable adaptive triggers and haptic feedback for a more immersive combat feel.

KEYBOARD & MOUSE SETUP (PC PLAYERS)

For those playing on keyboard and mouse, remapping keys for faster combos and reaction times is highly recommended:

1. Go to Settings → Keybinds

2. Set important keys close together (e.g., Dodge = Shift, Attack = Left Click, Special = Right Click)

3. Adjust Mouse Sensitivity for precise camera movement.

4. If needed, enable Controller Support for a smoother experience.

STEP 3: SETTING UP SOUND & AUDIO PREFERENCES

BLEACH: Rebirth of Souls features high-quality voice acting, explosive battle sounds, and a nostalgic anime soundtrack. Setting up your audio mix can enhance immersion:

1. Go to Settings → Audio

2. Adjust the following:

   o Master Volume: Keep at 100% or adjust based on preference.

   o Music Volume: Lower slightly if you want to focus on in-game sounds.

   o Voice Volume: Increase to hear dialogue during cutscenes and battles.

   o Surround Sound (For Headphones/Surround Systems): Enable for 360° directional sound—perfect for catching enemy movements.

   o Subtitles: Turn ON if you prefer reading dialogue while playing.

STEP 4: SETTING UP ONLINE & MULTIPLAYER PREFERENCES

If you're planning to take your skills online, a few network settings will ensure smooth matchmaking and stable connections:

1. Go to Settings → Online Options

2. Configure:

   ○ Matchmaking Region: Set to the closest region for lower ping and reduced lag.

   ○ Crossplay (If Available): Enable if you want to battle players from all platforms or disable to stick with your console.

   ○ Ping Display: Turn ON to monitor your connection stability.

   ○ Voice Chat: Choose On/Off based on whether you want to communicate with teammates/opponents.

For best performance, use a wired internet connection instead of Wi-Fi to reduce lag spikes and disconnects during battles.

STEP 5: CHECKING FOR UPDATES & BONUS CONTENT

Before you start playing, make sure you're running the latest game version:
On PC (Steam/Epic Games) – Go to Library → Right Click on Game → Check for Updates.
On PlayStation/Xbox – Navigate to Game Options → Check for Updates.

Also, if you pre-ordered or purchased special editions, now is the time to redeem exclusive DLC content, such as:

- Bonus Characters (e.g., Pre-order Ichigo Variant)

- Alternative Costumes

- Exclusive Battle Arenas

FINAL STEP: ENTER THE BATTLEFIELD!

Once you've completed your first-time setup, you're officially ready to begin your journey as a Soul Reaper, Arrancar, or Quincy. Whether you're jumping into Story Mode, Training, or Online Battles, you're now fully prepared to experience *BLEACH: Rebirth of Souls* at its best.

Now go forth, unleash your Bankai, and dominate the battlefield!

2.4 TROUBLESHOOTING COMMON ISSUES

Even the most polished games can come with technical hiccups, and *BLEACH: Rebirth of Souls* is no exception. Whether you're dealing with installation errors, performance drops, crashes, or online connectivity issues, this troubleshooting guide will help you quickly identify and resolve problems so you can get back to dominating battles.

ISSUE #1: GAME WON'T LAUNCH OR CRASHES ON STARTUP (PC & CONSOLE)

POSSIBLE CAUSES & FIXES

PC Users:

- Check System Requirements – Ensure your PC meets the minimum or recommended specs (See Section 2.1).

- Run as Administrator – Right-click the game icon and select Run as Administrator to bypass permission issues.

- Verify Game Files – Corrupted files can prevent the game from launching.

    - Steam: Library → Right-click game → Properties → Installed Files → Verify Integrity of Game Files.

    - Epic Games: Library → Click the three dots next to the game → Verify.

- Update GPU Drivers – Go to NVIDIA GeForce Experience or AMD Radeon Software and update your graphics drivers.

- Disable Overlays – Close apps like Discord, GeForce Overlay, or Xbox Game Bar, as they can interfere with launching.

Console Users (PS4/PS5/Xbox):

- Check for Updates – Outdated game versions can cause crashes.

    - PS: Highlight the game → Options → Check for Update.

    - Xbox: My Games & Apps → Manage → Updates.

- Clear Cache – Restart your console and hold the power button for 10 seconds to clear temporary files.

- Reinstall the Game – If all else fails, delete and reinstall the game to ensure clean installation.

ISSUE #2: LOW FPS OR STUTTERING (PC ONLY)

POSSIBLE CAUSES & FIXES

Lower Graphics Settings

- If FPS drops occur, navigate to Settings → Graphics and adjust:

    o Lower Shadows & Texture Quality

    o Disable Ray Tracing (if applicable)

    o Enable DLSS (NVIDIA users) or FSR (AMD users)

    o Set FPS Limit to 60+ for smoother gameplay

Close Background Apps

- Task Manager (Ctrl+Shift+Esc) → End unnecessary tasks like browsers, Discord, or recording software

Switch to Performance Mode (PS5/Xbox Series X)

- Console players can enable Performance Mode to prioritize FPS over graphics in the system settings.

Ensure Laptop is Running on High Performance Mode

- Windows Settings → Power & Battery → Select High Performance Mode.

ISSUE #3: MULTIPLAYER CONNECTION ISSUES (LAG, DISCONNECTS, UNABLE TO FIND MATCHES)

POSSIBLE CAUSES & FIXES

Check Your Internet Connection

- Run a speed test (speedtest.net) – You need at least 5-10 Mbps upload/download speed for stable online matches.

- Use Wired Connection – A LAN cable is more stable than Wi-Fi.

Matchmaking Issues

- Change Region Settings – Go to Settings → Online Options and select a closer matchmaking server.

- Enable/Disable Crossplay – Some players find quicker matches by either turning on or off crossplay in settings.

NAT Type Problems (Xbox & PlayStation Only)

- If you see a "Strict" NAT Type, it can prevent multiplayer access. Fix this by:
    - Restarting your router
    - Enabling UPnP (Universal Plug and Play) in your router settings
    - Using a wired connection instead of Wi-Fi

ISSUE #4: GAME FREEZES, AUDIO GLITCHES, OR GRAPHICAL BUGS

POSSIBLE CAUSES & FIXES

Restart Your System

- Simply restarting your PC or console can fix temporary bugs.

Check for Game Updates & Patches

- Developers often release hotfixes for issues like audio desync, UI glitches, and texture pop-ins.

- Check Steam, PlayStation Store, or Xbox Store for patches.

Disable Unnecessary Features

- For audio glitches, go to Settings → Audio and:

    o Lower sound effects volume slightly.

    o Switch between Stereo and Surround Sound modes.

    o If using Bluetooth headphones, try wired headphones instead.

Reinstall the Game (As a Last Resort)

- If nothing works, a fresh reinstallation might resolve deep-rooted game file issues.

ISSUE #5: CONTROLLER NOT WORKING (PC USERS ONLY)

POSSIBLE CAUSES & FIXES

Check Controller Support in Steam

1. Steam → Settings → Controller → Enable Support for PS/Xbox Controllers

2. Restart the game and try again.

Use Wired Connection Instead of Bluetooth

- If the controller lags or disconnects, try plugging it in directly via USB-C or Micro-USB cable.

Reconfigure Button Mapping

- Go to Settings → Controls → Reset to Default or Customize Bindings.

FINAL STEP: CONTACT SUPPORT (IF ALL ELSE FAILS)

If you've tried all solutions and still face major issues, reach out to:
Game Support Website: (Check the official website for *BLEACH: Rebirth of Souls*).
 Steam/Epic Support: (For PC version troubleshooting).
PlayStation/Xbox Support: (For console-related errors).

FINAL VERDICT: KEEP THE BATTLES RUNNING SMOOTHLY!

Technical issues can be frustrating, but most of them have quick fixes. With this troubleshooting guide, you're now equipped to solve common problems and get back into the action without delay.

Now, go out there, master your Zanpakutō, and dominate the battlefield!

CHAPTER 3: UNDERSTANDING GAMEPLAY MECHANICS

3.1 BASIC CONTROLS AND UI NAVIGATION

Mastering the controls and user interface (UI) in *BLEACH: Rebirth of Souls* is the first step to becoming a true warrior. Whether you're a casual player looking for smooth gameplay or an advanced fighter aiming for precise combos, understanding the mechanics will give you a solid foundation to dodge, attack, and unleash powerful Bankai transformations with ease.

MASTERING THE BASIC CONTROLS

Each platform has its own default control scheme, but all of them follow a similar combat flow—attack, defend, evade, and use abilities. Below is a quick breakdown of the basic controls for PlayStation, Xbox, and PC players.

PLAYSTATION & XBOX CONTROLS

Action	PlayStation (PS4/PS5)	Xbox (One/Series X/S)
Light Attack	□ (Square)	X
Heavy Attack	△ (Triangle)	Y

Dodge/Step	X (Cross)	A
Jump	O (Circle)	B
Guard/Block	L1	LB
Special Ability	R1	RB
Ultimate Move (Bankai/Resurrection/Quincy Vollständig)	L2 + R2	LT + RT
Lock-On Target	R3 (Right Stick Click)	R3 (Right Stick Click)
Switch Targets	Right Stick (Tilt)	Right Stick (Tilt)
Dash/Sprint	L3 (Left Stick Click)	L3 (Left Stick Click)
Use Assist Character (if applicable)	L1 + R1	LB + RB

Pro Tip:

- Light Attacks are faster but deal less damage, while Heavy Attacks take longer but hit harder.

- Dodge and Guard wisely—some attacks can't be blocked!

- Lock onto enemies to maintain pressure in fights.

KEYBOARD & MOUSE CONTROLS (PC PLAYERS)

Action	Default Key (PC)

Light Attack	Left Click
Heavy Attack	Right Click
Dodge/Step	Spacebar
Jump	Shift
Guard/Block	Q
Special Ability	E
Ultimate Move (Bankai/Resurrection/Volls tändig)	R
Lock-On Target	Tab
Switch Targets	Mouse Wheel (Scroll)
Dash/Sprint	Left Shift
Use Assist Character (if applicable)	F

Pro Tip:

- If you're playing on PC, consider remapping controls for comfort, especially if you're using a keyboard instead of a controller.
- Adjust mouse sensitivity in settings for precise camera movement.

UI NAVIGATION & UNDERSTANDING THE HUD

The User Interface (UI) and Heads-Up Display (HUD) in *BLEACH: Rebirth of Souls* are designed to give you all the information you need while keeping the screen uncluttered for intense battles.

COMBAT HUD (HEADS-UP DISPLAY)

Health Bar (Top Left or Center)

- Your character's health—if it reaches zero, you lose the battle.

- Some characters have regeneration abilities, but most will need to avoid damage strategically.

◆ Spirit Energy Gauge (Below Health Bar)

- Used for Special Moves, Dashes, and Flash Steps (Shunpo/Sonído/Blut).

- Recharges over time or by attacking/blocking enemy attacks.

Ultimate Meter (Bankai/Vollständig Gauge – Bottom Right)

- When fully charged, you can unleash your most powerful transformation (Bankai, Resurrection, Vollständig, etc.).

- Charge it by landing attacks, taking damage, or manually charging (if applicable).

Lock-On Indicator (Centered on Screen)

- Shows which enemy you're targeting.

- If an enemy is about to unleash a strong attack, the indicator may flash red as a warning.

✕⏷ Assist Character Icon (If Available)

- Some game modes allow you to call in an Assist Character for extra attacks or defensive maneuvers.

- The icon will show when they are ready to be summoned.

MAIN MENU & GAME MODES NAVIGATION

When you start the game, you'll navigate through different menus to choose game modes, customize characters, and access settings.

Main Menu Options:
Story Mode – Play through the main BLEACH storyline with iconic battles.
Arcade Mode – Battle against AI in quick fights or tournaments.
Multiplayer (Online & Local) – Fight ranked or casual matches against real players.
Training Mode – Test combos, master characters, and refine skills.
5️⃣ Character Customization – Change outfits, abilities, and settings.
6️⃣ Options & Settings – Adjust graphics, audio, and control settings.

Pro Tip:

- If you're new, start with Training Mode to get a feel for the controls before jumping into intense fights.

- Story Mode can unlock new characters and rewards, so consider playing through it before heading to Multiplayer.

MASTERING THE UI AND CONTROLS FOR COMBAT SUCCESS

Now that you understand the controls and UI, you're one step closer to becoming a legendary Soul Reaper. Whether you're learning the basics or refining advanced techniques, mastering these fundamentals will elevate your gameplay and make every fight feel smooth and intuitive.

Next up—let's dive deeper into character roles, abilities, and fighting mechanics! Get ready to step up your game!

3.2 COMBAT SYSTEM AND ATTACK TYPES

The combat system in *BLEACH: Rebirth of Souls* is a blend of strategy, reflexes, and power management. Battles are fast-paced, requiring players to balance offense and defense, time their attacks, and use abilities strategically to dominate their opponents. In this section, we break down the attack types, combat flow, and mechanics that will turn you from a novice fighter into a battle-hardened warrior.

CORE COMBAT SYSTEM OVERVIEW

The game follows a 3D arena fighting system, where players move freely within the battle zone while engaging in intense melee and ranged combat. Every character has a unique fighting style, but all share a core combat structure consisting of:

Light and Heavy Attacks – Standard offensive moves for chaining combos.
 Dashes and Dodges – Essential for evading enemy strikes.
 Blocks and Parries – Reducing or countering damage from incoming attacks.
 Special Abilities – Unique moves tied to a character's Zanpakutō, Hollow powers, or Quincy techniques.
 Ultimate Moves (Bankai, Resurrection, Vollständig, etc.) – Devastating finishers that can turn the tide of battle.

 Pro Tip: Mastering combos, dodging, and counter-attacks will set apart skilled fighters from button mashers!

ATTACK TYPES AND THEIR EFFECTS

Different attacks serve different combat purposes. Knowing when to use each type effectively can give you a huge advantage in battle.

LIGHT ATTACKS (QUICK STRIKES)

Fast and fluid attacks, useful for quick combos.
Low damage but excellent for staggering enemies.
Works well for chaining into special moves.

Best Used For:

- Fast opponents who rely on mobility.

- Setting up longer combos.

- Interrupting enemy attacks.

HEAVY ATTACKS (POWER STRIKES)

Slower but stronger than light attacks.
Some heavy attacks can break an opponent's guard.
Can launch enemies into the air for aerial combos.

Best Used For:

- Punishing enemies who are too aggressive.

- Breaking through blocks and defenses.

- Dealing massive damage in one hit.

GRAB ATTACKS (THROWS & GRABS)

Used to break blocking opponents.
Some characters have unique grab-based special moves.
Can be followed up with a quick strike or combo.

Best Used For:

- Defensive players who turtle behind blocks.

- Opponents who spam dodge moves (grabs ignore dodges if timed correctly).

RANGED ATTACKS (SPIRITUAL ENERGY BLASTS)

Typically weaker than melee attacks but safer from a distance.
Used by Quincy, Kido Users, and Hollow-based fighters.
Some ranged attacks can be charged for extra power.

Best Used For:

- Keeping distance from aggressive opponents.

- Forcing enemies to close the gap (making them predictable).

- Comboing into melee attacks for unpredictable pressure.

GUARDING, PARRYING & COUNTERS

Defense is just as important as offense! Master these mechanics to control the fight:

Guarding (Blocking) – Reduces or nullifies damage but can be broken by heavy attacks or grabs.

Parrying (Perfect Guarding) – If you block just before impact, you can stagger the attacker and counter.

Counters (Interrupt Moves) – Some characters have counter-attack abilities that punish aggressive foes.

Best Used For:

- Reading enemy attacks and responding accordingly.

- Turning defense into offense by punishing mistakes.

- Avoiding unnecessary damage in long fights.

COMBAT FLOW & ADVANCED TECHNIQUES

To truly master the combat system, you need to understand the flow of battle and execute advanced techniques.

COMBO CHAINS AND CANCELING

Chain light and heavy attacks to keep enemies on the defensive.
Use dash cancels (dodging mid-combo) to extend attacks.
Some characters have infinite combo loops (if timed correctly).

Example Basic Combo:
Light Attack → Light Attack → Heavy Attack → Dash Cancel → Special Move.

STAGGER AND JUGGLE MECHANICS

Some moves stagger opponents, leaving them open for more attacks.
Air juggles keep enemies suspended, allowing extended damage.

Best Used For:

- Pressuring opponents who don't block well.

- Maximizing damage output in every encounter.

FLASH STEP, SONÍDO, AND HIRENKYAKU (DASH TECHNIQUES)

Essential for dodging incoming attacks.
Used to quickly close distance or escape.
Some characters can chain multiple dashes for mobility advantages.

Best Used For:

- Evading special moves that deal heavy damage.

- Outmaneuvering slower opponents.

- Chasing down enemies trying to escape.

ULTIMATE ABILITIES & AWAKENING FORMS (BANKAI, RESURRECTION, VOLLSTÄNDIG, ETC.)

Available when the Ultimate Gauge is full.
Transformations give huge stat boosts and unique move sets.
Some ultimate moves are instant K.O. in specific conditions.

Best Used For:

- Comeback moments in close matches.

- Finishing off opponents before they can recover.

- Turning the tide of battle when at low health.

3.3 CHARACTER PROGRESSION AND LEVELING

In *BLEACH: Rebirth of Souls*, power isn't just about raw skill—it's about growth, adaptation, and unlocking your full potential. As you fight through battles, your character will gain experience, unlock new abilities, and level up, gradually becoming a more formidable warrior. This section covers everything you need to know about progression, experience points (XP), skill upgrades, and transformations so you can maximize your character's potential and dominate the battlefield.

HOW CHARACTER PROGRESSION WORKS

Every character in *BLEACH: Rebirth of Souls* follows a progression system that rewards players for continued play. Whether you're focusing on Story Mode, Arcade Battles, or Multiplayer, progression follows this core structure:

Earn XP – Gained through battles, completing objectives, and special challenges.
Level Up – XP fills the Level Progression Bar, unlocking new moves, stats, and abilities.
Unlock New Abilities – Special moves, transformations, and passive boosts become available.
Mastery & Special Forms – Higher-level characters gain access to advanced abilities and unique transformation mechanics.

Pro Tip: The more you experiment with different characters, the better you'll understand their strengths and weaknesses at each stage of progression.

EARNING XP AND LEVELING UP

HOW TO GAIN XP FAST

XP is earned differently across the various game modes. Here's how to maximize your gains:

Story Mode – Completing missions gives large XP boosts.
Arcade Mode – Fighting tougher AI opponents provides bonus XP.
Multiplayer Battles – XP scales with performance—winning faster and taking less damage gives more rewards.
Daily & Weekly Challenges – Special tasks that grant huge XP payouts for completing objectives.

Pro Tip:

- Higher difficulty modes give more XP but require better skills.

- Replaying tougher battles can be the fastest way to grind XP.

UNLOCKING ABILITIES AND POWER-UPS

Each character's progression tree is different, but most follow a similar skill-unlocking structure.

BASIC SKILL UNLOCKS (LEVELS 1-10)

New combos and attacks become available.
Slight stat boosts (Attack, Defense, Speed).
Small Spirit Energy increases for more abilities.

Best Strategy: Learn the fundamental combos early and get comfortable with character movement.

INTERMEDIATE GROWTH (LEVELS 11-30)

Unlock signature moves like Getsuga Tenshō (Ichigo), Cero Oscuras (Ulquiorra), and Senbonzakura (Byakuya).
Dodge, Counter, and Guarding improvements—reaction-based skills improve.
Enhanced Spirit Energy bar, allowing for longer special move chains.

Best Strategy: Start experimenting with different playstyles—learn offensive vs. defensive tactics.

ADVANCED GROWTH & SPECIAL FORMS (LEVELS 31-50+)

Unlock Ultimate Moves & Transformations (Bankai, Resurrection, Vollständig).
Higher damage resistance and mobility speed.
Access to new combo routes that extend attack chains.
Certain characters unlock alternative fighting styles (e.g., Ichigo's Hollow Mask).

Best Strategy: Transform strategically—wasting your Bankai or Resurrection too early could backfire!

MASTERING TRANSFORMATIONS (BANKAI, RESURRECTION, VOLLSTÄNDIG, ETC.)

One of the most exciting aspects of progression is unlocking your character's ultimate transformation. These power-ups enhance abilities, increase damage output, and unlock devastating finishers.

HOW TO UNLOCK TRANSFORMATIONS

Earn XP and level up to reach the required rank.
Some characters must complete specific story missions.
Spirit Energy Bar must be maxed before transforming in battle.

Best Used For:

- Turning the tide of battle when at low health.

- Activating before landing a powerful combo for insane damage.

- Countering enemy ultimates with your own power-up.

CHARACTER-SPECIFIC GROWTH PATHS

Each fighter in *BLEACH: Rebirth of Souls* follows a unique leveling path.
While some characters gain strength quickly, others require mastery over
time. Here's a quick breakdown:

POWER FIGHTERS (ICHIGO, KENPACHI, YAMAMOTO, GRIMMJOW)

High damage output but rely on close-range combat.
Transformations boost raw attack power.
Best suited for aggressive, fast-paced players.

Tip: Focus on strengthening attack power and unlocking high-damage
combos early.

SPEED & MOBILITY FIGHTERS (YORUICHI, SOIFON, STARRK, URYŪ ISHIDA)

Excel in dodging and counterattacking.
Damage is lower, but they can hit-and-run efficiently.
Special abilities favor quick strikes and mobility-based skills.

Tip: Focus on mobility upgrades—staying elusive is the key to survival.

TECHNICAL & KIDO USERS (AIZEN, URAHARA, BYAKUYA, TŌSEN, RUKIA)

Utilize Spiritual Energy-based attacks (Kido, illusions, projectiles).
Best at zoning out enemies and controlling space.
Can be tricky to master but reward smart playstyles.

Tip: Master ranged attacks and counterplays to dominate matchups against power fighters.

PRESTIGE LEVELS AND ENDGAME MASTERY

Once you max out your character's level, you unlock Prestige Ranks— allowing you to replay the leveling process with exclusive rewards.

Prestige Leveling resets your character's level but lets you keep certain unlocked abilities.
Each Prestige Rank unlocks new cosmetics, transformations, and battle enhancements.
Only the most dedicated players will reach max Prestige and master every character.

Best Strategy:

- If you're looking to fully master a character, Prestige is worth grinding.

- Some special moves and skins are only available at high Prestige levels.

3.4 SPECIAL ABILITIES AND POWER-UPS

In *BLEACH: Rebirth of Souls*, victory isn't just about basic attacks and dodging—it's about unleashing devastating abilities and tapping into powerful transformations that can change the course of battle in an instant. Every fighter has access to unique abilities based on their Zanpakutō, Hollow powers, Quincy techniques, or Kido mastery, making each character distinct in combat.

This section will break down the different types of special abilities, power-up mechanics, and how to maximize their effectiveness.

TYPES OF SPECIAL ABILITIES

Every character has three core categories of special abilities, each offering different advantages in battle:

Signature Moves – Unique attacks tied to a character's fighting style and lore.
Spirit Energy-Based Abilities – Kido, Cero, Getsuga Tenshō, and other ranged/magical attacks.
Transformation Power-Ups – Activating Bankai, Resurrection, Vollständig, or other ultimate forms.

Pro Tip: Special abilities use Spirit Energy, so managing your energy bar efficiently is just as important as knowing when to attack or defend.

SIGNATURE MOVES AND SPECIAL ATTACKS

Each character has at least one signature move that represents their unique combat style. These moves are often flashy, powerful, and require Spirit Energy to execute.

ZANPAKUTŌ-BASED ATTACKS (SHINIGAMI FIGHTERS)

Exclusive to Shinigami characters, involving sword-based techniques. Can be enhanced when a character reaches Shikai or Bankai.
Examples:

- Ichigo Kurosaki – Getsuga Tenshō (Energy Wave Attack).

- Byakuya Kuchiki – Senbonzakura (Blade Petal Barrage).

- Tōshirō Hitsugaya – Hyōrinmaru (Ice Dragon Strike).

Best Used For:

- Mid-range pressure to force opponents to play defensively.

- Finishing off weakened enemies with powerful bursts.

HOLLOW & ARRANCAR ABILITIES

Exclusive to Hollow and Arrancar characters, destructive and chaotic. Often involve Cero blasts, Sonído dashes, and brutal melee attacks.
Examples:

- Ulquiorra Cifer – Cero Oscuras (Dark Cero).

- Grimmjow Jaegerjaquez – Desgarrón (Energy Claws).

- Nnoitra Gilga – Hierro Guard (Super Armor Defense).

Best Used For:

- Close-range combat dominance.

- Overpowering defensive enemies with relentless pressure.

QUINCY TECHNIQUES & REISHI MANIPULATION

Unique to Quincy characters, focusing on ranged attacks and tactical movement.
Can absorb Spirit Particles to boost attacks.
Examples:

- Uryū Ishida – Licht Regen (Rapid Reishi Arrow Barrage).

- Jugram Haschwalth – The Balance (Damage Reflection).

- Yhwach – The Almighty (Prediction & Counterattack Boost).

Best Used For:

- Keeping enemies at a distance while controlling the battlefield.

- Setting traps and baiting opponents into counterattacks.

KIDO & SPELL-BASED TECHNIQUES

Used by Shinigami proficient in Kido and spiritual magic.
Can be defensive (barriers) or offensive (energy blasts, paralysis spells).
Examples:

- Sōsuke Aizen – Kyōka Suigetsu (Illusion Domination).

- Rukia Kuchiki – Sōren Sōkatsui (Double Energy Blast).

- Tessai Tsukabishi – Hadō 99: Goryūtenmetsu (Forbidden Spell).

Best Used For:

- Confusing and outmaneuvering opponents.

- Setting up devastating combos with immobilizing spells.

TRANSFORMATION POWER-UPS (BANKAI, RESURRECTION, VOLLSTÄNDIG, ETC.)

Transformations in *BLEACH: Rebirth of Souls* are game-changing power-ups that significantly enhance a character's abilities, stats, and move sets. These forms can turn the tide of battle, so timing their activation correctly is crucial.

HOW TO ACTIVATE TRANSFORMATIONS

Transformations require a full Spirit Energy Bar.
Some characters must take damage to unlock their awakening state.
Once activated, characters gain new abilities and higher stats for a limited time.

SHINIGAMI BANKAI (ULTIMATE SWORD RELEASE)

The most powerful transformation for Shinigami characters.
Unlocks new combos, stronger attacks, and increased speed.
Examples:

- Ichigo Kurosaki – Tensa Zangetsu (Enhanced Speed & Damage).

- Byakuya Kuchiki – Senbonzakura Kageyoshi (Mass Blade Storm).

- Tōshirō Hitsugaya – Daiguren Hyōrinmaru (Giant Ice Dragon Armor).

Best Strategy: Use Bankai at the right moment—wasting it too early can leave you vulnerable later.

ARRANCAR RESURRECTION (TRUE HOLLOW FORM RELEASE)

Exclusive to Hollow and Arrancar characters.
Regenerates health, boosts damage, and unlocks destructive attacks.
Examples:

- Ulquiorra Cifer – Segunda Etapa (Ultimate Form, Massive Power Increase).

- Grimmjow Jaegerjaquez – Pantera (Claw & Speed Enhancement).

- Barragan Louisenbairn – Arrogante (Decay-Based Abilities).

Best Strategy: Use Resurrection when at half health—the regeneration can help you survive longer.

QUINCY VOLLSTÄNDIG (HOLY FORM AWAKENING)

The ultimate power-up for Quincy characters.
Significantly increases Reishi control, mobility, and ranged attack power.
Examples:

- Uryū Ishida – Licht Regen Mastery (Rapid Fire Arrow Storm).

- Jugram Haschwalth – The Almighty Enhancement (Enhanced Prediction & Attack Reflection).

- Yhwach – Omnipotence Boost (God-Tier Reality Manipulation).

Best Strategy: Vollständig gives a huge power spike but is temporary—use it to finish fights quickly.

MAXIMIZING YOUR POWER-UPS IN COMBAT

Special Abilities + Power-Ups = Total Domination

Manage Spirit Energy Wisely – Using up your energy too fast leaves you vulnerable.
Know When to Transform – Don't waste Bankai or Resurrection early in battle.
Mix Signature Moves & Combos – Use special attacks within your combos for insane damage output.
Adapt to Your Opponent's Playstyle – If your enemy is dodging too much, use auto-targeting special moves.

CHAPTER 4: CHARACTER CLASSES AND PLAYSTYLES

4.1 SOUL REAPERS: STRENGTHS AND WEAKNESSES

Soul Reapers, also known as Shinigami, are one of the most versatile fighter classes in *BLEACH: Rebirth of Souls*. These warriors wield Zanpakutō (Soul-Cleaving Swords), master Kido spells, and unlock Bankai transformations that can turn the tide of battle.

Understanding their strengths and weaknesses is crucial if you want to maximize their potential or counter them effectively. This section breaks down everything you need to know about playing as a Soul Reaper or fighting against one.

STRENGTHS OF SOUL REAPERS

Balanced Playstyle – Soul Reapers excel in a mix of speed, power, and technique, making them adaptable to most combat situations.

Shikai & Bankai Transformations – As battles progress, Soul Reapers can unleash devastating power-ups, gaining new abilities and massive stat boosts.

Superior Mobility – With Shunpo (Flash Step), they can close gaps quickly, dodge enemy attacks, and reposition effectively.

Kido Techniques – Unlike some other classes, many Soul Reapers can use energy-based spells (Kido) for offense, defense, and utility.

Strong Defensive Capabilities – They can block, counter, and parry attacks more efficiently than Arrancars or Quincies.

Best Playstyle: If you enjoy fast-paced combat, flashy transformations, and diverse abilities, Soul Reapers are an excellent choice.

WEAKNESSES OF SOUL REAPERS

✖ Energy Management Issues – Using Bankai, Kido, and powerful abilities drains Spirit Energy quickly. Poor management leaves them vulnerable.

✖ Predictable Attack Patterns – Most Soul Reapers rely heavily on Zanpakutō-based combat, making them easier to counter if you know their move set.

✖ Transformation Reliance – While Bankai provides a major power boost, some fighters are far weaker before activating it.

✖ Struggle Against Ranged Opponents – Quincies and certain Arrancars can outrange Soul Reapers, forcing them to close the distance under fire.

Best Counterplay: Pressure them early, bait out their energy-based moves, and exploit their weaknesses before they can reach Bankai.

BEST SOUL REAPERS TO PLAY (TOP-TIER CHOICES)

Ichigo Kurosaki – Versatile powerhouse, combining speed, damage, and devastating Bankai attacks.
Byakuya Kuchiki – Deadly mid-range fighter with blade petals and high-level Kido.
Kenpachi Zaraki – Raw power, insane damage, but lacks ranged attacks.
Tōshirō Hitsugaya – Ice-based techniques, crowd control, and a deadly Daiguren Hyōrinmaru Bankai.

Sōsuke Aizen – Illusion-based deception and one of the most dangerous fighters in the game.

Best Strategy: Master Flash Step movement, Shikai abilities, and energy conservation to become an unstoppable Soul Reaper!

4.2 ARRANCARS: UNIQUE ABILITIES AND TACTICS

Arrancars are Hollows that have removed their masks, gaining Shinigami-like abilities while retaining their monstrous strength. These hybrid warriors blend brutal melee combat with devastating spiritual attacks, making them some of the most aggressive and unpredictable fighters in the game.

This section will break down their unique abilities, key strategies, and the best ways to play as or against them.

NIQUE ABILITIES OF ARRANCARS

Resurrección (Hollow Evolution) – Instead of Bankai, Arrancars activate Resurrección, transforming into their true forms and gaining a massive power boost.

Cero & Bala Attacks – Arrancars can fire energy-based attacks, such as Cero (massive blasts) and Bala (faster, weaker energy shots), to keep pressure on opponents.

Hierro (Iron Skin) – Many Arrancars have hardened skin that reduces incoming damage, making them tougher than Soul Reapers in direct combat.

Sonído (Flash Step Alternative) – Their version of Shunpo, allowing for high-speed movement and deceptive attack patterns.

Unpredictable Attack Styles – Arrancars are less traditional than Soul Reapers, often using brutal melee attacks mixed with high-energy bursts.

Best Playstyle: If you enjoy aggressive, relentless combat with powerful transformations, Arrancars are perfect for you.

TACTICS FOR DOMINATING AS AN ARRANCAR

Close the Distance – Arrancars excel in melee combat, so use Sonído dashes to get in fast and overwhelm ranged opponents.

Mix Up Attacks – Combine Cero blasts, melee combos, and unpredictable movement to keep your enemies guessing.

Resurrección Timing – Unlike Bankai, Resurrección provides instant regeneration and power boosts—activate it when you're low on health to surprise opponents.

Bait & Counter – Use Bala for quick attacks, then punish dodging opponents with heavy strikes.

Best Strategy: Stay aggressive, force your opponents on the defensive, and time your Resurrección for maximum impact.

WEAKNESSES OF ARRANCARS

✘ Reckless Playstyle – Many Arrancar abilities favor offense over defense, making them vulnerable to counterattacks.

✘ High Energy Consumption – Cero and Resurrección drain Spirit Energy rapidly, meaning mismanaging power can leave you exposed.

✘ Weak Against Skilled Defenders – Experienced Soul Reaper players can parry and counter many of their aggressive moves, neutralizing their offense.

✕ Predictable Power-Ups – Most Arrancars follow a similar pattern: pressure, transform, overwhelm. Skilled players can prepare for this and counter accordingly.

Best Counterplay: Outlast their aggression, punish their openings, and don't let them dictate the pace of the fight.

BEST ARRANCARS TO PLAY (TOP-TIER CHOICES)

Ulquiorra Cifer – One of the strongest fighters in the game, with his Segunda Etapa form making him nearly unstoppable.
 Grimmjow Jaegerjaquez – Speed-based brawler, specializing in relentless melee combos and devastating finishers.
 Starrk – Ranged specialist, using dual Cero guns and high-speed movement.
 Barragan Louisenbairn – Decay-based fighter, forcing opponents to stay away or suffer constant damage.
 Nnoitra Gilga – Toughest defense in the game, thanks to Hierro and long-reach melee attacks.

Best Strategy: Play aggressively, master Resurrección, and use Cero attacks wisely to control the fight.

4.3 QUINCY AND FULLBRINGERS: SPECIAL COMBAT TECHNIQUES

BLEACH: Rebirth of Souls features a diverse roster of fighters, and among them, Quincy and Fullbringers bring some of the most unique combat styles to the battlefield. These warriors rely on Reishi manipulation, ranged precision, and reality-altering abilities to dominate their opponents.

In this section, we'll break down their core mechanics, signature techniques, and strategic advantages so you can master their playstyles.

QUINCY: MASTERS OF REISHI MANIPULATION

The Quincy are spiritually aware humans who specialize in long-range combat and Reishi absorption. Unlike Soul Reapers, they don't use Zanpakutō—instead, they craft spirit weapons using the very energy around them.

QUINCY COMBAT STRENGTHS

Long-Range Combat Dominance – Quincy fighters excel at ranged attacks, keeping opponents at a safe distance while delivering precise damage.
Reishi Absorption – They can draw in spirit energy from their surroundings, replenishing their attacks faster than other classes.
Hirenkyaku (Quincy Flash Step) – Comparable to Shunpo and Sonído, but with even greater distance coverage and evasiveness.
Vollständig (Ultimate Form) – Similar to Bankai and Resurrección, but grants flight, enhanced arrows, and new abilities.

Best Playstyle: If you enjoy sniping, precision-based combat, and controlling the battlefield from a distance, Quincy fighters are your best bet.

KEY QUINCY TECHNIQUES

Spirit Bow & Reishi Arrows – The signature weapon of most Quincy, capable of rapid-fire attacks or charged, high-damage shots.
Blut Vene & Blut Arterie – A dual-power system where Blut Vene boosts defense, while Blut Arterie increases attack power.
Sklaverei (Reishi Domination) – Absorbs spiritual particles in the air, strengthening attacks or nullifying enemy abilities.
Vollständig (Holy Form Awakening) – A god-like transformation that massively boosts speed, damage, and spiritual control.

Best Strategy: Keep your enemies at bay, time your Vollständig activation wisely, and use Reishi absorption to maintain an advantage.

BEST QUINCY FIGHTERS TO PLAY

Uryū Ishida – Balanced playstyle, fast attacks, and adaptive counterattacks.
Jugram Haschwalth – Strong defensive capabilities with The Balance ability (reflects damage taken).
Bazz-B – Fire-based Quincy with explosive mid-range attacks.
Askin Nakk Le Vaar – Unique damage resistance abilities, making him difficult to kill.
Yhwach – The ultimate Quincy, with reality-bending powers and extreme damage output.

Best Strategy: Use your ranged attacks to zone out opponents, then finish them with a devastating Vollständig combo.

FULLBRINGERS: REALITY-WARPING BRAWLERS

Fullbringers are humans with unique powers that allow them to manipulate the souls within objects, granting them supernatural abilities. Unlike Quincies, Fullbringers focus on melee combat with environmental manipulation.

FULLBRINGER COMBAT STRENGTHS

Close-Range Power – Fullbringers specialize in hand-to-hand combat, enhanced physical strength, and speed-based fighting.
Soul Manipulation – They can change the properties of objects, such as making the ground springy, enhancing their weapons, or even shifting reality.
Superhuman Reflexes – Fullbringers have insane agility, allowing them to

dodge and counterattack fluidly.
Unique Abilities per User – Unlike Soul Reapers or Quincies, Fullbringers have wildly different abilities, making them unpredictable.

Best Playstyle: If you like fast-paced melee combat, environmental control, and flashy abilities, Fullbringers are for you.

KEY FULLBRINGER TECHNIQUES

Bringer Light (Super Speed) – Allows Fullbringers to move at extreme speeds, leaving afterimages to confuse enemies.
Object Soul Manipulation – Lets them enhance weapons, change terrain properties, or create defensive barriers.
Augmented Physical Strength – Their combat abilities surpass even some Shinigami in raw power.
Unique Awakening Modes – Some Fullbringers gain temporary power boosts that alter their fighting style completely.

Best Strategy: Use movement to stay unpredictable, manipulate the battlefield, and overpower opponents with rapid melee attacks.

BEST FULLBRINGER FIGHTERS TO PLAY

Kūgo Ginjō – All-around fighter with strong swordplay and energy-enhanced strikes.
Shūkurō Tsukishima – Deadly counterattacks, able to rewrite the past of any object or person.
Jackie Tristan – Power increases the dirtier she gets, making her stronger the longer she fights.
Giriko Kutsuzawa – Uses time-based abilities, creating explosive delays in attacks.

Best Strategy: Adapt your tactics mid-battle—use speed, power, and terrain manipulation to gain the upper hand.

QUINCY VS. FULLBRINGERS: WHO'S STRONGER?

Quincy = Long-range masters, energy manipulation, and defensive buffs.
Fullbringers = Close-range experts, environmental control, and high-speed movement.

Quincy win if they can keep their distance and outmaneuver Fullbringers with ranged attacks.
Fullbringers win if they can close the gap and overwhelm Quincies before they can charge their energy.

4.4 BEST CHARACTERS FOR DIFFERENT PLAYSTYLES

Different players thrive with different playstyles, so choosing the right character for your preferred combat approach is key. This section breaks down which fighters suit which playstyles, from aggressive rush-downs to defensive counter-fighters.

BEST CHARACTERS FOR RUSH-DOWN PLAYERS (AGGRESSIVE COMBATANTS)

Ideal for players who love constant pressure, overwhelming enemies with speed and power.

Ichigo Kurosaki – Fast-paced combat, balanced attack power, and strong transformation potential.
Grimmjow Jaegerjaquez – Relentless melee attacks, high-speed movement,

and brutal combos.

Kūgo Ginjō – Fullbringer with adaptive combat and explosive close-range power.

Kenpachi Zaraki – Pure brute force, thrives in aggressive, high-damage trades.

Best Strategy: Stay in your opponent's face, mix up attacks, and don't let them breathe.

BEST CHARACTERS FOR DEFENSIVE & COUNTER-ATTACK PLAYERS

Perfect for those who prefer waiting for openings and punishing mistakes.

Byakuya Kuchiki – Deadly at mid-range, zoning with Senbonzakura blade petals.

Tōshirō Hitsugaya – Ice-based crowd control, defensive techniques, and zone denial.

Jugram Haschwalth – Damage reflection and prediction-based counterattacks.

Shūkurō Tsukishima – Manipulates the past, setting up unpredictable counters.

Best Strategy: Play patient, let opponents overextend, then punish them hard.

BEST CHARACTERS FOR RANGED & TACTICAL PLAYERS

For players who love controlling space, sniping opponents, and setting up traps.

Uryū Ishida – Fast, long-range Quincy archer, excellent for zoning.
Starrk – Dual-pistol Cero attacks with massive range.

Askin Nakk Le Vaar – Poison-based damage and tricky survival tactics.
Barragan Loulsenbairn – Decay abilities force enemies to fight on his terms.

Best Strategy: Stay out of reach, force opponents to chase you, and punish them from a distance.

With these insights, you're now armed with the knowledge to pick the perfect fighter for your style!

CHAPTER 5: WEAPONS, EQUIPMENT, AND CUSTOMIZATION

5.1 ZANPAKUTO TYPES AND THEIR FUNCTIONS

In *BLEACH: Rebirth of Souls*, Zanpakutō (Soul Slayer swords) are the defining weapons of Soul Reapers, each possessing unique abilities and transformations. Understanding their different types and functions will give you an edge in battle, whether you're playing aggressively, defensively, or tactically.

This section explores the main Zanpakutō classifications, their combat applications, and how to harness their power effectively in the game.

THE THREE MAIN ZANPAKUTŌ TYPES

Zanpakutō are categorized into three primary types, each suited for different playstyles and combat strategies.

---

1. MELEE-TYPE ZANPAKUTŌ (FOR DIRECT COMBAT SPECIALISTS)

Melee-type Zanpakutō are designed for close-range combat, enhancing the wielder's physical abilities, attack speed, or cutting power.

High damage output in close quarters
Fast attack speed and strong combos

Varied abilities (enhanced slashes, shockwaves, energy-infused strikes, etc.)

Best for: Players who prefer aggressive, up-close fighting styles.

TOP MELEE-TYPE ZANPAKUTŌ

Zangetsu (Ichigo Kurosaki) – Excels in speed and raw power, capable of launching Getsuga Tenshō energy slashes.
Ryūjin Jakka (Genryūsai Yamamoto) – Fire-based Zanpakutō with immense destructive power.
Senbonzakura (Byakuya Kuchiki) – Can split into thousands of blade petals, useful for offense and defense.
Nozarashi (Kenpachi Zaraki) – Raw, unfiltered destruction, maximizing power at the cost of speed.

Best Strategy: Rush your enemies, keep up relentless pressure, and chain combos for devastating results.

2. KIDO-TYPE ZANPAKUTŌ (FOR MAGIC & ENERGY-BASED COMBAT)

Kido-type Zanpakutō harness spiritual energy to cast powerful abilities, focusing on ranged attacks, illusions, and elemental damage.

Excels in long-range and technical combat
Can trap, immobilize, or weaken enemies
Powerful special effects (fire, ice, poison, etc.)

Best for: Players who like tactical, ability-driven gameplay with magic-like mechanics.

TOP KIDO-TYPE ZANPAKUTŌ

Hyōrinmaru (Tōshirō Hitsugaya) – Ice-based Zanpakutō that can freeze opponents and control the battlefield.
Katen Kyōkotsu (Shunsui Kyōraku) – Creates deadly game-like conditions, where rules dictate combat outcomes.
Sakanade (Shinji Hirako) – Causes visual perception inversion, disorienting enemies completely.
Tobiume (Momo Hinamori) – Explosive fireballs for burn damage and area control.

Best Strategy: Keep your distance, cast powerful effects, and control enemy movements.

3. SPECIAL-TYPE ZANPAKUTŌ (FOR UNPREDICTABLE & HYBRID COMBAT)

Special-type Zanpakutō don't fit neatly into melee or Kido categories. Instead, they feature unique mechanics, from time manipulation to poison effects.

Unconventional fighting styles
Hard to predict, giving a strategic advantage
Often require deep mastery but highly rewarding

Best for: Players who love mind games, deception, and strategic combat approaches.

TOP SPECIAL-TYPE ZANPAKUTŌ

🔁 Kyōka Suigetsu (Sōsuke Aizen) – Complete hypnosis, forcing opponents into false perceptions.
🐍 Zabimaru (Renji Abarai) – Whip-like segments for extended melee combat.
☐ Suzumushi (Kaname Tōsen) – Creates a sound-based void, cutting off enemy senses.

Ashisogi Jizō (Mayuri Kurotsuchi) – Neurotoxin-based, paralyzing foes on contact.

Best Strategy: Confuse and mislead opponents while creating openings for decisive strikes.

MASTERING ZANPAKUTŌ RELEASES: SHIKAI & BANKAI

Every Zanpakutō has two evolutionary stages, significantly boosting its power.

Shikai – The first transformation, unlocking a stronger form and unique abilities.
Bankai – The ultimate form, offering massive power spikes and new mechanics.

Best Strategy: Time your releases wisely—activating Bankai too early could leave you vulnerable later in the fight.

With the right Zanpakutō, you can dominate the battlefield. Choose one that fits your style and wield it like a true warrior!

5.2 ARMOR AND ACCESSORIES FOR BATTLE ENHANCEMENT

Gear plays a crucial role in *BLEACH: Rebirth of Souls*, boosting stats, improving resistances, and enhancing combat effectiveness. Understanding which armor and accessories best suit your playstyle can make the difference between victory and defeat.

UNDERSTANDING ARMOR TIERS & RESISTANCES

Armor in the game follows a tiered system, with each set offering different stat boosts and resistances.

LIGHT ARMOR (FOR SPEED & AGILITY PLAYERS)

Enhances movement speed & dodge rate
Lowers stamina consumption for dashes
Best for aggressive and hit-and-run playstyles

Best for: Quincy, assassins, and fast Soul Reapers like Yoruichi Shihōin.

MEDIUM ARMOR (BALANCED DEFENSE & OFFENSE)

Decent mobility while still offering protection
Good balance of stamina and endurance
Effective for all-around fighters

Best for: Balanced Soul Reapers like Ichigo, Renji, and Grimmjow.

HEAVY ARMOR (FOR TANKY & DEFENSIVE PLAYSTYLES)

Highest defense and damage reduction
Absorbs powerful attacks with reduced knockback
Slower movement speed but better survivability

Best for: Tanky fighters like Kenpachi Zaraki and Yamamoto.

MUST-HAVE ACCESSORIES FOR BATTLE ENHANCEMENT

Equipping the right accessories can complement your playstyle, giving you an advantage in combat.

OFFENSIVE ACCESSORIES

Power Bands – Increases melee attack power.
Spiritual Amplifiers – Boosts Kido-based abilities.
Reishi Control Gauntlets – Enhances Quincy arrow speed and damage.

DEFENSIVE ACCESSORIES

Reiryoku Shields – Absorbs spiritual attacks.
Hardened Soul Bracers – Reduces stamina drain for blocking.
Resilience Charms – Lowers debuff effects (poison, paralysis, etc.).

UTILITY ACCESSORIES

Hōgyoku Shard – Shortens cooldowns for special abilities.
Sonído Boots – Enhances Flash Step distance.
Garganta Key – Faster respawn time in certain game modes.

BEST ARMOR & ACCESSORY COMBINATIONS FOR PLAYSTYLES

SPEED-BASED FIGHTERS (QUINCY, YORUICHI, SOI FON)

Light Armor + Sonído Boots + Power Bands

BALANCED FIGHTERS (ICHIGO, BYAKUYA, GRIMMJOW)

Medium Armor + Hōgyoku Shard + Spiritual Amplifier

TANKY DEFENDERS (KENPACHI, YAMAMOTO, BARRAGAN)

Heavy Armor + Reiryoku Shield + Resilience Charm

PRO TIP:

Match your armor and accessories to your playstyle—don't just equip the strongest gear, but the gear that complements your abilities.

With the right armor and accessories, you'll enhance your strengths, cover weaknesses, and dominate every battle!

5.3 HOW TO UPGRADE AND MODIFY EQUIPMENT

In *BLEACH: Rebirth of Souls*, raw skill can only take you so far—enhancing your gear is the key to staying ahead of the competition. Whether you're upgrading your Zanpakutō, reinforcing armor, or customizing accessories, mastering the upgrade system will give you a massive advantage in both PvE and PvP battles.

This section will cover how to upgrade your weapons and gear effectively, as well as the best modification strategies for different playstyles.

Equipment upgrades follow a tiered progression system, where each enhancement improves stats, unlocks special abilities, and boosts durability.

1. WEAPON UPGRADES: STRENGTHENING YOUR ZANPAKUTŌ

Zanpakutō can be upgraded in several ways, each affecting their damage, speed, and unique abilities.

UPGRADE METHODS:

Reiryoku Infusion – Enhances raw attack power, increasing damage per hit.
 Elemental Augmentation – Infuses the blade with fire, ice, lightning, or poison for status effects.
 Spiritual Resonance – Boosts special ability damage, making Shikai & Bankai even more powerful.
 Weight Reduction – Increases attack speed at the cost of slight damage reduction.

 Best Strategy: Customize your Zanpakutō to match your combat style— prioritize power for heavy hitters, speed for assassins, and elemental effects for crowd control.

2. ARMOR REINFORCEMENT: ENHANCING YOUR DEFENSE

Armor can be reinforced to increase durability, resistances, and special effects.

KEY REINFORCEMENT TYPES:

◆ Durability Upgrade – Increases damage resistance, allowing you to tank more hits.
◆ Reishi Fortification – Strengthens spiritual defenses, reducing energy-based damage.
◆ Mobility Enhancement – Lowers weight penalties, making it easier to dodge and move freely.
◆ Anti-Debuff Protection – Reduces the impact of poison, paralysis, and spiritual drain effects.

Best Strategy: Balance defense with mobility—too much armor can slow you down, but too little can leave you vulnerable.

3. ACCESSORY MODIFICATIONS: FINE-TUNING YOUR LOADOUT

Accessories can be modified with special enhancements, giving you combat perks and buffs.

TOP MODIFICATIONS:

Critical Strike Boost – Increases critical hit chance for more devastating attacks.
Energy Recovery Rate – Speeds up Reiatsu regeneration, allowing faster ability usage.
Cooldown Reduction – Shortens special ability cooldowns, making Shikai & Bankai more frequent.
Stealth Enhancements – Lowers detection range, perfect for assassins and ambush specialists.

Best Strategy: Stack mods that complement your playstyle—speed players should focus on mobility, while tanks should enhance resilience.

ADVANCED UPGRADE MATERIALS & HOW TO GET THEM

Higher-tier upgrades require rare materials, which can be obtained through:

Defeating Bosses – High-level enemies drop legendary crafting items.
Spirit Trials – Challenge missions that reward exclusive upgrade materials.
Ranked PvP Rewards – Competitive matches grant special enhancement orbs.
Fusion Crafting – Combining lower-tier materials to create high-tier enhancements.

Pro Tip: Focus on farming endgame bosses for the rarest upgrade materials—they make a huge difference in high-stakes battles.

By mastering the upgrade system, you'll turn good equipment into legendary gear, allowing you to crush opponents and dominate the battlefield.

Now that we've upgraded your gear, let's talk about optimizing loadouts for competitive play!

5.4 BEST LOADOUTS FOR COMPETITIVE PLAY

When it comes to high-level PvP and ranked matches, having the right loadout is just as important as skill. Choosing the right Zanpakutō, armor, and accessories can give you the edge you need to outplay your opponents.

This section breaks down the best loadouts based on different competitive playstyles.

LOADOUT 1: THE SPEED DEMON (HIT-AND-RUN PLAYSTYLE)

Zanpakutō: *Senbonzakura* (Byakuya Kuchiki) – Agile and excellent for quick slashes & zoning attacks.
Armor: *Lightweight Shinigami Robes* – Maximizes speed and dodge rate.
Accessories:
Sonído Boots – Boosts Flash Step distance.
Critical Strike Bands – Increases chance of fast, deadly hits.
Cooldown Reduction Charm – Faster access to special abilities.

Best Strategy: Stay mobile, avoid direct confrontations, and use speed to outmaneuver enemies.

LOADOUT 2: THE BRUISER (TANKY MELEE SPECIALIST)

Zanpakutō: *Nozarashi* (Kenpachi Zaraki) – Pure destructive power, ideal for heavy hits.
Armor: *Reinforced Captain's Armor* – High durability, excellent for absorbing damage.
Accessories:
◆ *Resilience Charm* – Reduces stun and knockback effects.
◆ *Reiryoku Shield* – Decreases incoming energy-based damage.
◆ *Power Bands* – Boosts melee attack strength.

Best Strategy: Tank hits, punish enemies with devastating strikes, and overwhelm them with raw power.

LOADOUT 3: THE ENERGY MASTER (KIDO-BASED FIGHTER)

Zanpakutō: *Hyōrinmaru* (Tōshirō Hitsugaya) – Ice-based, excellent for freezing enemies in place.
Armor: *Kido Master's Robes* – Enhances spiritual energy attacks.
Accessories:
Reiatsu Amplifier – Boosts Kido ability damage.
Energy Recovery Charm – Speeds up Reiatsu regeneration.
Cooldown Reduction Beads – Faster access to Kido attacks.

Best Strategy: Control the battlefield with ranged attacks and status effects—stay at a distance and wear enemies down.

LOADOUT 4: THE DECEPTION EXPERT (TRICKSTER & MIND GAMES)

Zanpakutō: *Kyōka Suigetsu* (Sōsuke Aizen) – Hypnosis-based, can completely disorient opponents.
Armor: *Silent Assassin's Garb* – Reduces visibility on radar, enhances stealth.
Accessories:
Stealth Enhancement Device – Hides presence from minimaps.
Illusionist's Charm – Confuses enemy targeting systems.
Speed Augmenter – Improves reaction time and movement speed.

Best Strategy: Mess with your opponents' perception—use illusions and stealth to create chaos and confusion.

CHAPTER 6: STRATEGIES AND EXPERT TIPS

6.1 HOW TO MASTER THE PARRY AND COUNTER SYSTEM

In *BLEACH: Rebirth of Souls*, timing is everything—a well-executed parry and counter can turn the tide of battle instantly. Mastering this system allows you to punish aggressive opponents, block devastating attacks, and create openings for deadly combos.

This section breaks down the mechanics of the parry system, how to counter effectively, and the best ways to use this technique against different enemy types and playstyles.

UNDERSTANDING THE PARRY SYSTEM

Parrying is not just about blocking—it's about redirecting the enemy's attack to create an advantage. When performed correctly, a parry:

Nullifies incoming damage (for most attacks).
Briefly staggers the attacker, leaving them open for a counter.
Builds up your special meter faster.
Can cancel out certain abilities, including powerful finishing moves.

However, mistiming a parry can be disastrous, leading to stun effects or taking full damage from an enemy's attack.

Key Tip: The parry window is small, so learning enemy attack patterns is crucial to success.

HOW TO EXECUTE A PERFECT PARRY

To parry successfully, follow these steps:

Anticipate the Attack – Watch your opponent's movements closely. Heavy attacks are easier to parry because they have longer wind-up animations.
Time Your Guard – Just before the attack makes contact, press the parry button (usually mapped to a dedicated block/parry key).
Confirm the Parry Effect – If successful, your character will glow slightly, and the enemy will stagger.
Execute a Counterattack – Follow up immediately with a quick strike or special ability while the opponent is vulnerable.

Pro Tip: Avoid spamming the parry button—mistiming can cause you to fail the block entirely, leaving you wide open.

ADVANCED PARRY TECHNIQUES

Once you've mastered basic parrying, take your skills to the next level with these advanced techniques:

1. PERFECT PARRY CANCELS

If you parry at the exact frame an attack lands, you can completely negate stagger and chain into an immediate attack.
This is extremely effective in PvP, where fast reactions can overwhelm your opponent.

2. PARRY INTO FLASH STEP COUNTER

After a successful parry, use Flash Step (Shunpo, Sonído, or Hirenkyaku) to dash behind the enemy and strike from an unexpected angle.

Works best against heavily armored opponents who take longer to
recover from stagger.

3. PARRY AGAINST SPECIAL ABILITIES

Some special moves can be parried, but the timing is much stricter.
Experiment with different enemy abilities in training mode to master
parry windows for each attack.

BEST CHARACTERS FOR PARRY & COUNTER PLAYSTYLE

Certain characters excel at parry-based combat due to their high-speed
counters and stagger abilities.

Byakuya Kuchiki – *Senbonzakura* has a quick draw counter that follows up
with a petal barrage.
Sajin Komamura – His parry stun duration is longer, giving him better
counter windows.
Ichigo Kurosaki (Final Getsuga Tenshō Form) – Gains Reiatsu regeneration
when successfully parrying an attack.

Best Strategy: Pick characters with strong counters and fast execution to
maximize parry effectiveness.

Mastering the parry and counter system makes you nearly untouchable in
battle, allowing you to turn enemy aggression into your advantage. Now,
let's explore how to dodge and move effectively to avoid getting hit
altogether!

6.2 EFFECTIVE DODGING AND
MOVEMENT TECHNIQUES

Dodging is just as important as attacking in *BLEACH: Rebirth of Souls*—a well-timed evade can save you from one-shot attacks, while advanced movement techniques allow you to position yourself for optimal damage output.

This section covers the fundamentals of dodging, the best evasive maneuvers, and movement tricks to outmaneuver any opponent.

THE BASICS OF DODGING

Dodging isn't just about getting out of the way—it's about positioning yourself to counterattack or escape danger.

Short Dodge (Quick Step) – A fast sidestep that allows you to evade light attacks.
 Long Dodge (Backstep Flip) – A backflip that creates more space, great against heavy attacks.
 Directional Evade (Side Flash Step) – A lateral dash that can reposition you behind the enemy.

 Best Strategy: Use different dodge types based on the situation—don't just rely on backsteps!

ADVANCED DODGING TECHNIQUES

1. I-FRAME DODGE (INVINCIBILITY FRAMES)

Some dodges have invincibility frames (i-frames) where you are completely immune to damage.
 Learning which frame the i-frame activates can let you evade unblockable attacks perfectly.

2. FLASH STEP CANCELS (SHUNPO, SONÍDO, HIRENKYAKU TECHNIQUES)

After dodging, quickly perform a Flash Step to reposition.
Works well against long-range opponents who try to track your movements.

3. DASH FAKE-OUTS (BAITING THE ENEMY)

Pretend to rush forward, then dash sideways at the last second.
Can be used to bait out attacks, leaving enemies vulnerable.

4. WALL RUNNING & AERIAL DODGES

Some characters can run along walls or perform aerial dodges, allowing them to escape tricky situations.
This is especially useful in multi-level maps with vertical movement options.

BEST CHARACTERS FOR DODGE-HEAVY PLAYSTYLES

Certain characters are built for mobility and excel at dodging rather than blocking.

Yoruichi Shihōin – Unmatched speed, with faster dodges than any other character.
Grimmjow Jaegerjaquez – Can chain dodges into aggressive counters.
Tōshirō Hitsugaya – Aerial mobility lets him escape ground-based attacks easily.

Best Strategy: If your character is built for speed, avoid blocking entirely and rely on dodging to win fights!

6.3 Understanding Enemy Attack Patterns

In *BLEACH: Rebirth of Souls*, knowing how enemies attack is just as important as knowing how to fight. Whether you're up against AI-controlled bosses or real PvP opponents, understanding attack patterns allows you to predict, counter, and dominate battles.

This section breaks down the key attack patterns of different enemy types, how to recognize warning signs, and the best strategies to react effectively.

THE THREE MAIN ATTACK CATEGORIES

All enemies in *Rebirth of Souls* follow one of three attack styles, and each requires a different defensive response:

Light Attacks – Fast, chainable strikes that don't deal massive damage but can break your guard over time.
Heavy Attacks – Slower, more powerful strikes that stagger or knock you back if you don't evade.
Unblockable Attacks – Special moves with red or purple warning indicators that cannot be parried or blocked—you must dodge or counter them.

Best Strategy: Learn which attacks can be blocked and which must be dodged to avoid unnecessary damage.

RECOGNIZING ENEMY PATTERNS

Most enemies follow a predictable pattern, with clear signs before they strike. By recognizing animation cues, you can react ahead of time instead of just relying on reflexes.

1. ATTACK STARTUP CUES (TELEGRAPHED ATTACKS)

Bosses and elite enemies have distinct wind-up animations before heavy or special attacks.
 Look for weapon glow effects (blue for strong attacks, red for unblockables).
 Voice lines or charging stances often indicate an incoming ultimate attack.

2. REPEATED COMBOS (PATTERN LOOPS)

Many enemies have set combos that they repeat with slight variations.
 If an enemy slashes twice, expect a third hit or a delayed strike.
 Some bosses change their patterns after losing health, becoming more aggressive or unpredictable.

3. FAKE-OUT ATTACKS (BAITING MOVES)

Advanced enemies may fake a swing, then delay their actual attack to catch impatient players.
 PvP opponents love to use fake-outs—wait until they fully commit before dodging.

STRATEGIES FOR COUNTERING DIFFERENT ENEMY TYPES

Different enemy types require different counter strategies:

LARGE & SLOW ENEMIES (*EXAMPLE: HOLLOWS & MENOS GRANDE*)

Parry their slow swings, then counter with strong attacks.
Circle around them—most have limited tracking.
Aim for weak points (glowing spots or exposed areas).

FAST & AGGRESSIVE ENEMIES (*EXAMPLE: ARRANCARS & QUINCY FIGHTERS*)

Don't try to block every hit—use dodges instead.
Interrupt their combos with quick strikes.
Bait them into attacking, then counter when they overextend.

BOSS CHARACTERS & PVP OPPONENTS

Learn their ultimate moves—every boss has a signature attack you can predict.
Save your strongest abilities for counterattacks—don't waste them early.
Adapt on the fly—high-level bosses and skilled players adjust their patterns mid-battle.

THE BEST WAY TO LEARN ATTACK PATTERNS

Use Training Mode – Practice reading attack patterns against AI-controlled enemies.
Watch Other Players – Observing PvP matches or high-level

gameplay videos helps you spot trends.
 Fight the Same Enemy Multiple Times – Each battle teaches you something new.

 Best Tip: The more you fight, the easier it becomes to predict and react!

Mastering enemy attack patterns puts you in complete control of fights—now, let's move on to the most effective battle strategies for PvP and PvE!

6.4 ADVANCED BATTLE STRATEGIES FOR PVP AND PVE

Now that you know how enemies fight, it's time to dominate every battle with pro-level strategies. Whether you're crushing AI bosses in PvE or outplaying human opponents in PvP, these advanced techniques will elevate your combat skills to the next level.

BEST STRATEGIES FOR PVE (SINGLE-PLAYER & CO-OP MODES)

PvE battles are about efficiency—you need to eliminate enemies quickly while minimizing damage taken.

---

1. MANAGE YOUR STAMINA WISELY

Don't waste stamina on excessive dodging—you'll be vulnerable when you run out.
 Save stamina for burst damage phases—some bosses expose weak points for only a few seconds.

Equip accessories that boost stamina regeneration to extend your fighting time.

2. PRIORITIZE WEAKER ENEMIES FIRST

In battles with multiple opponents, eliminate the weaker enemies first to avoid distractions.
Some small enemies buff bosses—take them out ASAP to prevent difficulty spikes.

3. USE ENVIRONMENTAL ADVANTAGES

Some maps have objects that block enemy attacks—use them to your advantage.
Ledges & high ground give you better visibility and can force melee enemies to chase you.

4. LEARN WHEN TO RETREAT

If your health is low, don't blindly attack—fall back, heal, and reassess.
Bosses often have desperation attacks when their HP is low—stay cautious!

BEST STRATEGIES FOR PVP (ONLINE BATTLES & RANKED PLAY)

PvP is all about mind games—you must outthink your opponent rather than just out-fight them.

1. READ YOUR OPPONENT'S HABITS

Does your opponent dodge too often? Time your attacks to hit when they land.

Do they spam a certain move? Learn to bait it out and counterattack.
Do they panic under pressure? Stay aggressive and force mistakes.

2. MASTER THE ART OF BAITING

Pretend to leave an opening, then counter when they attack.
Walk instead of running to make your opponent think you're vulnerable.
Cancel attack animations to fake a move, then strike when they react.

3. KNOW WHEN TO ENGAGE & WHEN TO PLAY DEFENSIVE

Aggressive play works against defensive opponents—overwhelm them with non-stop attacks.
Defensive play works against reckless opponents—punish their mistakes with precise counters.
Mix up your style so your opponent can't predict your next move.

4. ADAPT TO DIFFERENT PLAYSTYLES

Ranged Fighters (Quincy, Fullbringers) – Use Flash Step to close the gap quickly.
Heavy Attackers (Kenpachi, Komamura) – Dodge right before their attacks land to counter.
Speedsters (Yoruichi, Ichigo, Grimmjow) – Stay unpredictable to avoid getting overwhelmed.

BONUS PRO TIPS FOR PVP & PVE SUCCESS

Mind your cooldowns – Don't spam your strongest moves early—save them for game-changing moments.
Use the right character for the situation – Some characters excel in PvP, while others are better for PvE.

Don't panic under pressure – Staying calm lets you react properly, while panicking leads to bad decisions.

Experiment & practice – The best players are always learning new strategies to stay ahead of the competition.

CHAPTER 7: MISSION WALKTHROUGHS AND LEVEL GUIDES

7.1 BEGINNER MISSIONS AND HOW TO COMPLETE THEM

Starting out in *BLEACH: Rebirth of Souls* can feel overwhelming, but the beginner missions are designed to introduce core mechanics, build your confidence, and prepare you for tougher battles ahead. This section breaks down each beginner mission, highlights key objectives, and provides tips to complete them efficiently.

UNDERSTANDING BEGINNER MISSIONS

The first few missions serve as a tutorial phase, guiding you through:
 Basic movement & controls – Flash Step, guarding, and attacking.
 Combat fundamentals – Light and heavy attacks, special abilities, and Zanpakuto techniques.
 Character progression – How leveling up works and the benefits of upgrading abilities.
 Resource gathering – Collecting in-game currency, skill points, and items.

 Best Strategy: Treat beginner missions as a learning experience, not just something to rush through. The skills you refine here will help you dominate later stages.

MISSION 1: THE SOUL REAPER'S FIRST TEST

Objective: Defeat a group of low-level Hollows in Karakura Town.
This is a simple combat introduction. Use basic attacks and dodges to eliminate the enemies.
Practice parrying—you'll need it later!
Explore the area—there are hidden items to collect.

MISSION 2: AWAKENING YOUR ZANPAKUTO

Objective: Learn about your character's weapon and abilities.
You'll unlock your Zanpakuto's first ability here—experiment with it.
Try out different attack combinations to see what flows best.
Pay attention to stamina management—it becomes crucial in PvP and boss fights.

MISSION 3: DEFENDING THE HUMAN WORLD

Objective: Stop an enemy invasion before time runs out.
First timed mission—you must defeat enemies quickly.
Use area-of-effect (AoE) moves to handle groups of Hollows.
Don't waste time chasing enemies—let them come to you and strike efficiently.

MISSION 4: TRAINING WITH RENJI ABARAI

Objective: Spar against a mentor and learn advanced techniques.
Renji will block a lot—learn to mix up your attacks to break his guard.
Experiment with Flash Step to evade his Bankai attacks.
This mission tests everything you've learned so far—don't rely on button-mashing!

Practice combos early – The better your attack flow, the smoother your fights will be.

Use every ability at least once – Learn what works best for your playstyle.

Explore the map – There are hidden XP boosts and minor power-ups scattered around.

Get comfortable with dodging – You'll need it when facing stronger enemies later.

Once you've mastered the beginner missions, you're ready to tackle mid-game challenges and truly test your combat skills!

7.2 MID-GAME CHALLENGES AND STRATEGIES

Now that you've grasped the basics, the mid-game introduces stronger enemies, tougher mission conditions, and more strategic battles. This section will help you overcome new challenges, optimize your strategy, and continue progressing smoothly.

WHAT CHANGES IN THE MID-GAME?

Once you reach mid-game missions, expect:

Stronger enemies with unpredictable attack patterns

Longer fights that require stamina and cooldown management

More complex mission objectives (e.g., time limits, protection tasks, survival challenges)

Elite enemy encounters that introduce status effects

Best Strategy: By now, you should have a preferred character and fighting style—start refining your techniques instead of relying on basic attacks.

MISSION TYPE 1: BOSS FIGHTS (VS. NAMED CHARACTERS)

Expect characters like Grimmjow, Tōsen, or Hitsugaya as mid-game bosses.
Watch their move patterns—they use Bankai or Resurrección mid-fight.
Conserve your strongest abilities for their second phase.
If a boss enters Hyper Armor mode, stop attacking and focus on dodging until it ends.

MISSION TYPE 2: TIME-LIMITED CHALLENGES

You must defeat enemies before the timer runs out.
Use AoE attacks—they're the fastest way to clear groups.
Stay mobile—wasting time chasing enemies will cost you the mission.

MISSION TYPE 3: SURVIVAL WAVES

Enemies come in waves—you must last until the final wave.
Save healing items—don't waste them early on.
Manage stamina wisely—you don't want to be exhausted in the final wave.
Some waves include mini-bosses—defeat them quickly before more enemies spawn.

MISSION TYPE 4: ESCORT & PROTECTION TASKS

You must keep an NPC or object safe while enemies attack.
Position yourself between the target and enemies to intercept attacks.
Control the battlefield—push enemies away using knockback moves.
Some enemies ignore you and focus on the target—take them out first!

BEST STRATEGIES TO DOMINATE MID-GAME MISSIONS

Upgrade your abilities regularly – By now, you should have skill points—use them!

Focus on dodging rather than blocking – Enemies hit harder now; dodging is often safer.

Use Zanpakuto abilities wisely – Don't waste your ultimate attacks on weak enemies.

Experiment with different characters – Some missions may be easier with a ranged fighter instead of melee.

Keep an eye on enemy weaknesses – Some enemies are weak to certain Zanpakuto types.

Once you've mastered these mid-game challenges, you're ready for late-game missions, hidden boss fights, and elite endgame content!

7.3 BOSS FIGHTS AND HOW TO BEAT THEM

Boss fights in *BLEACH: Rebirth of Souls* are some of the most challenging and rewarding battles in the game. These powerful enemies have unique attack patterns, devastating abilities, and multiple phases, requiring a mix of skill, strategy, and patience to defeat.

This section breaks down key boss fights, their mechanics, and the best strategies to take them down efficiently.

UNDERSTANDING BOSS FIGHT MECHANICS

Most bosses in *Rebirth of Souls* follow a three-phase system, where they change their attack behavior as their health drops.

PHASE 1: TESTING YOUR SKILLS

The boss uses basic attacks to gauge your reactions.

Dodging and parrying are crucial—if you struggle here, you'll suffer in later phases.

Some bosses may use one special attack to catch you off guard.

PHASE 2: POWER SURGE & NEW MOVES

Bosses unlock stronger abilities (Bankai, Resurrección, Vollständig, etc.).

Expect faster attacks, new combos, and area-wide damage moves.

Aggressive bosses become relentless, while defensive bosses set traps.

PHASE 3: FINAL STAND (HYPER MODE)

This is when bosses go all out, often triggering a Hyper Armor phase where they take reduced damage.

Some bosses unleash unblockable ultimate attacks—recognize the warning signs and react accordingly.

Your goal is to outlast this phase—don't waste all your stamina too early.

Best Strategy: Learn when to attack, when to dodge, and when to back off. Many bosses punish over-aggression.

BREAKDOWN OF KEY BOSSES AND HOW TO DEFEAT THEM

BOSS: SOSUKE AIZEN (FINAL BATTLE – SOUL SOCIETY ARC)

Abilities: Kido spells, sword slashes, hypnosis-based feints.

Strategy:

Watch out for Kyoka Suigetsu illusions—Aizen fakes attacks to bait dodges.

Don't attack blindly—if he disappears, he's behind you.

When he enters Bankai mode, stay mid-range and counter when he recovers from long animations.

BOSS: ULQUIORRA CIFER (RESURRECCIÓN SEGUNDA ETAPA)

Abilities: High-speed attacks, energy lances, Cero Oscuras.
Strategy:
Stay mobile! Ulquiorra is one of the fastest bosses in the game.
When he flies into the air, get ready to dodge his Cero Oscuras.
Close-range characters struggle here—ranged fighters have an advantage.

BOSS: SAJIN KOMAMURA (HUMAN FORM & BANKAI MODE)

Abilities: Heavy melee strikes, armor-based defense.
Strategy:
Blocking won't work well—his attacks break guards easily.
Wait for his heavy slams, then counterattack during his cooldown.
If he summons his Giant Bankai Avatar, dodge behind it to avoid frontal slashes.

BOSS: GRIMMJOW JAEGERJAQUEZ (PANTHER MODE)

Abilities: Lightning-fast combos, panther-style rush attacks.
Strategy:
Don't let him corner you—he excels in close quarters.
When he glows red, get ready for a hyper-speed claw combo—dodge, don't block!
His rage mode drains stamina—force him to miss attacks to tire him out.

Final Tip: Each boss has weak points and recovery windows—study their animations and exploit their mistakes!

7.4 POST-GAME CONTENT AND SPECIAL CHALLENGES

Defeating the final boss doesn't mean the journey is over. *BLEACH: Rebirth of Souls* features post-game content that pushes players to their limits with:
 Secret bosses & hidden fights
 Ultimate difficulty missions
 Online PvP rankings
 New unlockable characters & skills

If you want to fully complete the game, here's what awaits you in the post-game phase.

SECRET BOSS FIGHTS & HIDDEN BATTLES

After beating the main storyline, you unlock new optional fights. These battles feature legendary BLEACH characters, each with special mechanics and no mercy.

SECRET BOSS: YHWACH – THE ALMIGHTY KING

Abilities: Future sight, instant counters, Reishi manipulation.
 Unlock Condition: Complete all Quincy-related story missions.
 Strategy:
 His "The Almighty" ability allows him to predict your attacks. Use feints to trick him.
 When he absorbs Reishi, interrupt him immediately. If you don't, he heals back to full.
 Never fight him head-on—bait him into attacking first, then counter.

SECRET BOSS: ICHIGO KUROSAKI (FINAL MUGETSU FORM)

Abilities: Getsuga Tensho waves, infinite Flash Step, high aggression.
Unlock Condition: Beat the game on Hard Mode.
Strategy:
His speed is unmatched—don't try to outspeed him, focus on countering.
His Final Getsuga Tensho is an instant KO if it lands—dodge at the last second.
Use terrain to your advantage—forcing him into small spaces limits his movement.

Tip: These fights are brutal but rewarding—you'll need maxed-out abilities and expert-level reflexes.

ULTIMATE DIFFICULTY MISSIONS

Once you complete the game, a new difficulty mode unlocks, featuring:
Enemies with higher health & damage
Stronger AI with adaptive attack patterns
Limited healing & resources

These missions are not for the faint of heart, but they reward rare gear, exclusive abilities, and bragging rights.

ONLINE PVP & RANKED BATTLES

Ready to test your skills against real players? Post-game mode lets you:
Compete in ranked PvP battles for leaderboard rewards.
Join a faction (Soul Reapers, Arrancars, Quincies, or Fullbringers) to earn exclusive bonuses.
Unlock hidden PvP-exclusive moves and character skins.

Best PvP Strategy: Adapt to your opponent's playstyle—no two players fight the same way.

UNLOCKABLE CHARACTERS & ULTIMATE ABILITIES

The post-game lets you unlock new characters, including:
 Hikone Ubuginu – A hybrid Soul with multi-race abilities.
 Aizen (Final Evolution) – Unlocks the Kanseikan form with near-invincibility.
 Urahara Kisuke (Final Bankai Form) – A highly technical character with insane counterattacks.

New Ultimate Abilities like:
 Hogyoku Resurrection (Aizen) – Grants temporary immortality.
 True Bankai (Renji) – Transforms attacks into ranged explosions.
 Quincy Schrift Activation (Haschwalth) – Reverses all damage taken for a limited time.

CHAPTER 8: SECRETS, COLLECTIBLES, AND HIDDEN CONTENT

8.1 UNLOCKABLE CHARACTERS AND COSTUMES

One of the most exciting aspects of *BLEACH: Rebirth of Souls* is the unlockable characters and alternate costumes. While the base roster includes fan-favorite characters, hidden fighters and outfits can be unlocked through gameplay achievements, challenges, and special conditions.

This section breaks down how to unlock secret characters, their special abilities, and exclusive costumes that enhance your style on the battlefield.

HOW TO UNLOCK SECRET CHARACTERS

Most unlockable characters fall into three main categories:
Story-Based Unlocks – Characters obtained by progressing through the main game.
Challenge-Based Unlocks – Fighters that require completing difficult tasks.
Event/Secret Unlocks – Hidden characters obtained through special conditions.

Here's how to unlock some of the most powerful hidden characters:

ICHIGO KUROSAKI (TRUE BANKAI FORM)

Unlock Condition: Complete the game on Hard Mode.
Abilities:
Final Getsuga Tensho – A devastating, full-screen energy slash.
Hyper-Speed Flash Step – Increased mobility for quick counters.

Tip: This form of Ichigo excels in aggressive combat but has low stamina recovery. Master dodging to compensate.

SOSUKE AIZEN (HOGYOKU EVOLUTION FORM)

Unlock Condition: Defeat Aizen in the Secret Boss Battle without taking more than 50% damage.
Abilities:
Immortal Regeneration – Passively heals over time.
Kanseikan Reality Warp – Temporarily negates all enemy attacks.

Tip: Aizen is a high-skill character—his abilities require precise timing to dominate fights.

SAJIN KOMAMURA (HUMAN FORM)

Unlock Condition: Complete all Survival Mode waves without dying.
Abilities:
Bankai: Kokujo Tengen Myo'o – Summons a giant warrior for heavy melee strikes.
Unbreakable Guard – Reduces all incoming damage by 30%.

Tip: Komamura's defensive playstyle makes him great for newer players looking to survive tough battles.

ULQUIORRA CIFER (SEGUNDA ETAPA FORM)

Unlock Condition: Win 10 consecutive PvP Ranked Matches.
Abilities:
Lanza del Relámpago – Throws an explosive energy spear.
Enhanced Cero Oscuras – A charged-up blast with armor-breaking properties.

Tip: Ulquiorra's long-range potential makes him a nightmare in PvP. Stay mobile and control spacing!

ALTERNATE COSTUMES AND HOW TO UNLOCK THEM

Costumes not only change a character's appearance but sometimes add minor stat boosts or special effects.

BEST ALTERNATE COSTUMES & HOW TO GET THEM

Ichigo (Hollow Mask Form) – Increases attack power by 10%.
How to Unlock: Complete the game on Normal Mode.

Rukia (Shinigami War Outfit) – Reduces skill cooldowns by 15%.
How to Unlock: Defeat 500 enemies using Rukia.

Aizen (White Suit Form) – Enhances Kido abilities.
How to Unlock: Clear all boss fights without using healing items.

Byakuya (Casual Outfit) – A visual-only change with no stat buffs.
How to Unlock: Win 50 PvP matches.

8.2 EASTER EGGS AND HIDDEN LOCATIONS

Like any great game, *BLEACH: Rebirth of Souls* is packed with Easter eggs, hidden references, and secret locations for players to discover. Some of these pay tribute to the BLEACH anime and manga, while others offer in-game rewards for those curious enough to explore.

HIDDEN EASTER EGGS & REFERENCES

Here are some of the best Easter eggs hidden throughout the game:

ICHIGO'S BEDROOM (KARAKURA TOWN)

Where to Find It: In Karakura Town, enter Ichigo's house and inspect his desk.
Easter Egg: A hilarious nod to Kon, where the stuffed lion complains about Ichigo leaving him behind.

Bonus: Interacting with the desk unlocks a secret voice line from Ichigo.

ISSHIN KUROSAKI'S SECRET TRAINING ROOM

Where to Find It: Inside the Kurosaki Clinic basement.
Easter Egg: A reference to Ichigo's hidden training session with his father, Isshin.

Bonus: Visiting this area unlocks a unique cutscene featuring Isshin giving combat advice.

ORIHIME'S COOKING DISASTER (COMEDY EASTER EGG)

Where to Find It: In Orihime's apartment.
 Easter Egg: Clicking on the stove triggers a funny animation where she tries to cook a dish that explodes.

 Bonus: Unlocks a food-related voice line from Uryu Ishida, where he criticizes Orihime's cooking.

KENPACHI'S DUEL CHALLENGE

Where to Find It: In Soul Society, enter the Eleventh Division Barracks and talk to Ikkaku.
 Easter Egg: Ikkaku invites you to spar with Kenpachi, triggering one of the hardest optional fights in the game.

 Bonus: Winning this fight unlocks Kenpachi's Eyepatch-Off Mode, increasing his attack damage in battle.

SECRET TRIBUTE TO BLEACH'S CREATOR, TITE KUBO

Where to Find It: Hidden within the Hueco Mundo wastelands.
 Easter Egg: A subtle tribute to BLEACH's creator—a gravestone with the initials "T.K." engraved on it.

 Bonus: This location also contains a rare Zanpakuto blueprint for crafting a legendary weapon.

Beyond Easter eggs, the game features hidden areas that reward players with rare items, special fights, and unique lore pieces.

THE ROYAL PALACE (SOUL KING'S DOMAIN)

How to Access: Must collect all 5 Spirit Keys scattered across the game.
Rewards: A secret mission where you battle Squad Zero for exclusive gear.

THE FORBIDDEN FOREST (HUECO MUNDO'S DEPTHS)

How to Access: Explore the darkest parts of Hueco Mundo at night.
Rewards: Unlocks a hidden boss fight against a mysterious Vasto Lorde.

ANCIENT RUKONGAI RUINS

How to Access: Complete all side missions in Soul Society.
Rewards: Secret lore cutscenes explaining Soul Society's ancient history.

8.3 SECRET ACHIEVEMENTS AND REWARDS

In *BLEACH: Rebirth of Souls*, achievements go beyond simple milestones—they unlock exclusive rewards, including hidden characters, special gear, and powerful in-game bonuses. While some achievements are straightforward, secret achievements require extra effort, exploration, or meeting special conditions.

This section breaks down the hardest-to-find achievements and how to unlock them, ensuring you get the full experience of the game.

"THE ULTIMATE SHINIGAMI" – UNLOCK ICHIGO'S FINAL FORM

Requirement: Complete Story Mode on Insane Difficulty without using continues.
  Reward: Ichigo (Final Getsuga Tensho Form) + Special Victory Animation.

Pro Tip: Master dodging and counterattacks to survive the toughest fights.

"AIZEN'S GRAND SCHEME" – WIN A BATTLE WITHOUT TAKING DAMAGE

Requirement: Win one full fight in any mode without getting hit.
  Reward: Aizen's White Suit Costume and a custom victory quote.

Pro Tip: Play defensively using parries, flash steps, and zoning attacks.

"KENNY'S BLOODLUST" – WIN WITH 1% HP REMAINING

Requirement: Defeat an opponent while on the verge of death.
Reward: Kenpachi removes his eyepatch permanently, boosting attack power.

Pro Tip: Try this against weaker enemies to unlock it more easily.

"THE HOLLOW WITHIN" – DEFEAT 100 ENEMIES USING HOLLOW FORMS

Requirement: Win 100 battles using characters in their Hollow transformations.
 Reward: Unlocks Ichigo's Full Hollow Mode and Ulquiorra's Segunda Etapa Form in all modes.

Pro Tip: Set up quick matches in Arcade Mode for faster progress.

"KING OF HUECO MUNDO" – DEFEAT ALL ESPADA IN BOSS RUSH MODE

Requirement: Defeat all Espada members in Boss Rush Mode without dying.
 Reward: Grimmjow's Pantera Form + Special Finishing Move.

 Pro Tip: Upgrade your stamina recovery and mobility to survive this brutal challenge.

"ZERO SQUAD CHALLENGER" – DEFEAT SQUAD ZERO IN A SECRET FIGHT

Requirement: Find and fight Squad Zero in The Royal Palace (Secret Area).
 Reward: Exclusive Squad Zero Armor Set with stat boosts.

Pro Tip: You must collect 5 Spirit Keys hidden throughout the game to access this fight.

"THE THOUSAND-YEAR WARRIOR" – WIN 500 ONLINE MATCHES

Requirement: Achieve 500 wins in Ranked PvP.
 Reward: Unlocks Yhwach (The Almighty Form) + Unique Combat Dialogue.

Pro Tip: Experiment with different character loadouts to counter opponents.

SECRET REWARDS & UNLOCKABLES

Aside from achievements, *BLEACH: Rebirth of Souls* hides powerful rewards for those who explore every aspect of the game.

Secret Weapon: *Yamamoto's Ryujin Jakka* (Strongest Fire-Based Zanpakuto)
Unlock by: Defeating Yamamoto in Secret Battle Mode without getting burned.

♥ Hidden Accessory: *The Hogyoku* (Boosts All Stats by 10%)
Unlock by: Completing Survival Mode (100 Waves) without dying.

Bonus Costume: *Hollow Mask Ichigo (Alternate Design)*
Unlock by: Performing 100 successful counters in battle.

8.4 HOW TO MAXIMIZE COMPLETION RATE

For true completionists, *BLEACH: Rebirth of Souls* offers a 100% completion goal, covering:

Story Mode
 Side Quests & Secret Bosses
 Achievements & Trophies
 Character Unlocks
 Costumes & Customizations
 All PvP & PvE Challenges

If you're aiming for total mastery, follow these key strategies to maximize completion rate efficiently.

STEP 1: PRIORITIZE STORY MODE & SIDE MISSIONS

Before diving into advanced challenges, finish Story Mode on Normal difficulty to unlock core characters and features.

Focus on:
 Completing ALL story missions.
 Checking side quests for hidden bosses & secret locations.
 Unlocking extra cutscenes & lore details.

Pro Tip: Finishing Story Mode unlocks tougher challenges but also gives better rewards for preparation.

STEP 2: MASTER COMBAT MECHANICS & PVP STRATEGIES

To complete the hardest achievements, you must master combat at every level.

Key skills to practice:
Parries & Counters – Needed for secret achievements.
Character-Specific Combos – Some fights require mastery of unique movesets.
PvP Tactics – Online matches unlock rare skins, XP boosts, and secret characters.

Pro Tip: Test different characters in Arcade Mode before committing to harder challenges.

STEP 3: TRACK ACHIEVEMENTS & SECRET UNLOCKS

Instead of randomly grinding, make a checklist of all achievements and secret conditions.

Checklist for 100% Completion:
Unlock ALL playable characters.
Collect ALL alternate costumes.
Complete ALL PvE challenges (Survival Mode, Boss Rush).
Earn ALL trophies & achievements (including hidden ones).
Win 100+ PvP matches for exclusive skins.

Pro Tip: Focus on one goal at a time—trying to unlock everything at once can slow your progress.

STEP 4: USE THE RIGHT LOADOUTS FOR CHALLENGES

Some achievements and fights require optimized builds to complete efficiently.

Best Loadouts for 100% Completion:

ATTACK-FOCUSED (BEST FOR PVP & BOSS FIGHTS)

Character: Ichigo (Final Bankai) / Aizen (Hogyoku Form)
Gear: Attack-boosting Zanpakuto + Speed-enhancing accessories
Strategy: Rushdown tactics, fast counters, and aggressive pressure.

DEFENSE/SURVIVABILITY (FOR HARD CHALLENGES & SECRET BOSSES)

Character: Yamamoto / Unohana / Kenpachi
Gear: HP-boosting armor + stamina recovery items
Strategy: Parry-heavy approach, endurance tactics, and strong counters.

BALANCED LOADOUT (BEST FOR EXPLORATION & GENERAL PLAY)

Character: Rukia / Toshiro / Urahara
Gear: Energy regeneration + special ability cooldown reduction
Strategy: Zoning tactics, quick movement, and adaptable combat.

Pro Tip: Some secret boss fights require specific characters to unlock hidden cutscenes & achievements!

STEP 5: TACKLE THE HARDEST CHALLENGES LAST

Once you've unlocked everything else, focus on the hardest challenges last:

Survival Mode (100 Waves) – Requires patience & skill.
Secret Bosses – Some fights take multiple attempts.
Ultimate PvP Rank – The toughest online test.

Pro Tip: Save your strongest characters & best gear for these final challenges.

Reaching 100% completion in BLEACH: Rebirth of Souls is a rewarding but challenging journey. Whether you're unlocking secret fighters, mastering PvP, or collecting rare achievements, following this strategy ensures you dominate the game.

Now, let's dive into Chapter 9: Achievements and Trophies, where we'll explore the full list of rewards you can earn!

CHAPTER 9: ACHIEVEMENTS, TROPHIES, AND COMPLETION GUIDE

9.1 FULL LIST OF ACHIEVEMENTS AND TROPHIES

Achievements in *BLEACH: Rebirth of Souls* are not just for bragging rights—they unlock exclusive content, from powerful characters to rare in-game items. Whether you're playing on PC, PlayStation, or Xbox, this section provides a complete list of trophies and achievements, categorized by difficulty.

Trophy Categories:
Bronze – Basic Achievements (Easy)
Silver – Mid-Tier Challenges (Medium)
Gold – Advanced Challenges (Hard)
Platinum – 100% Completion (Ultimate)

BRONZE ACHIEVEMENTS (BEGINNER-FRIENDLY, 10G / BRONZE TROPHY)

First Step to Power – Complete the tutorial.
Welcome to Soul Society – Clear the first Story Mode chapter.
Unleash Your Power! – Activate a Bankai, Resurrection, or Vollständig for the first time.
Combo Starter – Perform a 10-hit combo in battle.
Flash Step Master – Dodge 10 attacks in a row without getting hit.
The First Victory – Win a match in any game mode.
Collector's Spirit – Equip a new Zanpakuto or accessory.

Side Quest Enthusiast – Complete your first side mission.

Weapon Specialist – Win a fight using only Zanpakuto-based attacks.

Defense is Key – Successfully parry five consecutive attacks.

SILVER ACHIEVEMENTS (INTERMEDIATE, 25G / SILVER TROPHY)

Awakening the Beast – Unlock and use a Hollowfication ability in battle.

Climbing the Ranks – Reach Rank B in Ranked PvP.

Limit Breaker – Deal 500,000 damage in a single battle.

Legendary Rivalry – Win a 1v1 battle between Ichigo and Aizen.

Perfect Timing – Perform a Perfect Parry against a boss attack.

The Power of Bonds – Win a team battle with all characters still standing.

Reiatsu Overflow – Execute a 50-hit combo in battle.

No Holding Back – Defeat an opponent using only special abilities.

Espada Exterminator – Defeat all Espada members in Battle Mode.

Unstoppable Force – Win 10 battles in a row without losing.

GOLD ACHIEVEMENTS (DIFFICULT CHALLENGES, 50G / GOLD TROPHY)

King of Hueco Mundo – Clear Boss Rush Mode without losing a match.

The Final Bankai – Unlock Ichigo's Final Getsuga Tensho Form.

Survivor of 100 Battles – Complete 100 waves in Survival Mode.

Unmatched Power – Win 50 Ranked PvP Matches.

Speed Demon – Clear Story Mode on Hard Difficulty in under 6 hours.

The Unbreakable Wall – Block and counter 50 consecutive attacks in a battle.

The Ultimate Fighter – Achieve S-Rank in every mission.

Squad Zero's Test – Defeat Squad Zero in a secret fight.

Master of All Forms – Unlock every transformation (Bankai, Resurrección, Vollständig, etc.).

Battle Veteran – Play 200 matches in any game mode.

"The True Soul King" – Unlock all achievements/trophies in the game.

Reward: Exclusive Soul King's Cloak & Custom Title in PvP Mode.

Pro Tip: Only the most dedicated players will achieve this! It requires mastery of every mode, character, and battle strategy.

9.2 HOW TO UNLOCK DIFFICULT ACHIEVEMENTS

Some achievements require serious skill, time, and strategy to unlock. Here's how to conquer the most challenging ones in *BLEACH: Rebirth of Souls*!

KING OF HUECO MUNDO (DEFEAT ALL ESPADA IN BOSS RUSH MODE)

Requirement: Win against all Espada members in Boss Rush Mode without dying.
Reward: Unlock Grimmjow's Pantera Form + Special Finisher Animation.

How to Unlock It:
Use speed-based characters (Ichigo, Soi Fon, or Yoruichi) for better dodging.
Save your strongest moves for Ulquiorra Segunda Etapa and Barragan.
Equip stamina-boosting accessories to last longer in fights.

THE FINAL BANKAI (UNLOCK ICHIGO'S FINAL GETSUGA TENSHO FORM)

Requirement: Complete Story Mode on Insane Difficulty.
Reward: Unlock Ichigo's Final Form + Exclusive Ultimate Attack.

How to Unlock It:
Play defensively and master perfect parries.
Use a fully upgraded character with maxed-out skills.
Focus on counterattacks and mobility over raw offense.

SURVIVOR OF 100 BATTLES (COMPLETE 100 WAVES IN SURVIVAL MODE)

Requirement: Win 100 consecutive battles in Survival Mode.
Reward: Unlock The Hogyoku (Ultimate Power Boost Accessory).

How to Unlock It:
Use a high-defense character like Kenpachi or Yamamoto.
Manage stamina carefully—don't overuse Flash Steps.
Save Ultimate Moves for tougher waves (like Espada Bosses).

UNMATCHED POWER (WIN 50 RANKED PVP MATCHES)

Requirement: Win 50 matches in Online Ranked Mode.
Reward: Unlock Yhwach (The Almighty Form).

How to Unlock It:
Master at least two different characters to handle different matchups.
Learn advanced cancel techniques for chaining combos.
Play strategically—adapt to opponent playstyles mid-match.

SPEED DEMON (CLEAR STORY MODE ON HARD IN UNDER 6 HOURS)

Requirement: Complete Story Mode (Hard Difficulty) in under 6 hours.
Reward: Unlock Tensa Zangetsu as a Usable Zanpakuto.

How to Unlock It:
Skip cutscenes to save time.
Use a speed-based character like Soi Fon or Ichigo.
Focus on critical missions—avoid unnecessary side content until later.

THE TRUE SOUL KING (UNLOCK ALL ACHIEVEMENTS)

Requirement: Earn every single trophy/achievement.
Reward: Unlock Soul King's Cloak + Custom PvP Title.

How to Unlock It:
Follow a 100% completion guide to track progress.
Train in both PvP and PvE to master all game mechanics.
Stay consistent—some achievements require long-term dedication.

nlocking the toughest achievements in *BLEACH: Rebirth of Souls* is a true test of skill, patience, and mastery. Whether you aim to dominate PvP, conquer Survival Mode, or clear every story mission, these strategies will help you achieve 100% completion!

9.3 TIPS FOR 100% COMPLETION

Completing *BLEACH: Rebirth of Souls* 100% requires more than just finishing the main story. You need to unlock all characters, complete every side mission, collect rare items, and master difficult achievements. Below are pro-level tips to help you reach full completion and claim the ultimate rewards.

STEP 1: MASTER EVERY GAME MODE

To achieve 100% completion, you must finish all major game modes, including:

Story Mode – Complete every difficulty level.
Survival Mode – Reach Wave 100 to unlock exclusive rewards.
Boss Rush Mode – Defeat all major bosses without dying.
Ranked PvP – Win 50+ ranked matches to unlock online trophies.

Pro Tip: Start with Normal difficulty, then move up to Hard and Insane once you're comfortable.

STEP 2: COMPLETE EVERY SIDE QUEST AND CHALLENGE

Many rare characters, weapons, and secret cutscenes are locked behind side missions.

Faction Missions – Completing missions for Soul Reapers, Arrancars, and Quincies unlocks unique rewards.
Legendary Battles – Secret fights like Ichigo vs. Aizen (Final Battle) give special trophies.
Character Bond Events – Some characters unlock bonus abilities if you complete their side stories.

Pro Tip: Keep an eye on limited-time events, as they often feature exclusive rewards.

STEP 3: COLLECT EVERY ITEM AND UNLOCKABLE

To hit 100%, you'll need to find all collectibles:

Zanpakuto Variants – Unlock all alternate weapon skins.
Costumes – Obtain every character outfit, including DLC exclusives.
Easter Eggs – Discover hidden locations that reference the anime/manga.

Achievements & Trophies – Complete every challenge to earn the Platinum Trophy (or 1000G on Xbox/PC).

Pro Tip: Some rare items only appear on Hard or Insane difficulty, so replay missions as needed.

STEP 4: MAX OUT EVERY CHARACTER

To be a true completionist, you need to fully upgrade every character:

Max Level – Each character has a level cap. Train in Survival Mode for fast XP.
Skill Trees – Unlock all abilities and transformations.
Best Loadouts – Equip the most powerful Zanpakuto, armor, and accessories.
PvP Ranking – Reach the highest PvP rank (Soul King Tier) for an elite title.

Pro Tip: Some characters require specific battle conditions to unlock, so check the requirements early.

STEP 5: OPTIMIZE YOUR PLAYSTYLE FOR SPEED & EFFICIENCY

Use Speedrun Strategies – Skip non-essential fights and focus on fast clears.
Balance Offense & Defense – Some enemies require parrying and countering instead of brute force.
Experiment with Different Teams – Some missions are easier with specific character combinations.
Replay Key Missions – Some fights have multiple outcomes based on choices you make.

Pro Tip: Once you've mastered combat mechanics, try Hard Mode Speedruns to complete objectives faster.

100% COMPLETION REWARD:

Unlock "True Soul King" Title + Secret Cinematic Ending
Exclusive Zanpakuto Skin: Yhwach's Almighty Blade
Custom Player Card for Online PvP

9.4 UNLOCKING SECRET ENDINGS AND ALTERNATE PATHS

BLEACH: Rebirth of Souls features multiple endings, based on choices you make during the main story and certain battles. Unlocking them all requires specific actions and character interactions.

THE THREE MAIN ENDINGS

ENDING 1: "THE TRUE SOUL REAPER" (DEFAULT ENDING)

Requirement: Complete the game on any difficulty.
Outcome: Ichigo and the Soul Reapers defeat the main antagonist, restoring peace.

How to Unlock It: Simply finish the game normally.

ENDING 2: "THE PATH OF DARKNESS" (VILLAIN ENDING)

Requirement: Make certain choices that favor Hollows and Arrancars.
Outcome: The player aligns with the dark side, leading to a different final boss fight.

How to Unlock It:
Side with Aizen and Yhwach in key dialogue choices.

Defeat Byakuya and Yamamoto without sparing them.
Complete "The Hollow's Revenge" secret mission.

Exclusive Reward: Unlock Aizen (Final Form) as a playable character.

ENDING 3: "BEYOND THE SOUL KING" (SECRET ENDING)

Requirement: Complete the game on Insane Difficulty + Collect all secret items.
Outcome: A new, mysterious force is revealed, teasing a future battle beyond the Soul King's power.

How to Unlock It:
Win all boss fights without dying.
Unlock and equip the Hogyoku accessory before the final battle.
Find and activate all five Soul King Relics hidden across the game.

Exclusive Reward: Unlock Ichigo's Final Divine Bankai + Hidden Arena Mode.

HIDDEN BOSS FIGHTS & ALTERNATE BATTLE OUTCOMES

Certain fights have alternate outcomes, depending on how you play.

Yhwach vs. Ichigo Final Duel – If you survive for 5 minutes without using a Bankai, you trigger a secret ending dialogue.
Aizen's Betrayal Scene – Choose to spare or defeat Aizen after the final battle to unlock extra cutscenes.
Secret Boss: Squad Zero – If you finish the game with a 100% completion rate, you unlock a fight against Squad Zero, the strongest warriors of Soul Society.

POST-GAME UNLOCKABLES

New Game+ Mode – Keep all weapons, skills, and unlocked characters for a harder challenge.

Secret PvP Arenas – Unlock new battle stages from the anime/manga.

Custom Character Creator – Earn the ability to design your own Soul Reaper or Arrancar.

CHAPTER 10: ADDITIONAL RESOURCES AND COMMUNITY ENGAGEMENT

10.1 BEST ONLINE FORUMS AND COMMUNITIES FOR PLAYERS

In the fast-paced world of *BLEACH: Rebirth of Souls*, staying connected with the player community can give you the latest strategies, character tier lists, balance updates, and hidden secrets. Whether you're a beginner seeking guidance or a seasoned player looking for competitive matchups, these top forums and communities will keep you ahead of the game.

THE BEST BLEACH: REBIRTH OF SOULS COMMUNITIES

1. OFFICIAL BLEACH: REBIRTH OF SOULS DISCORD SERVER

Best for: Real-time discussions, character builds, PvP matchmaking, and patch news.
Why Join?

- Direct access to game developers and moderators.

- Find PvP sparring partners and form online squads.

- Get early leaks on upcoming DLCs and character updates.

How to Join: Look for the official invite link on the game's website or social media pages.

2. REDDIT – R/BLEACHREBIRTHOFSOULS

Best for: Theory-crafting, meme discussions, PvE tips, and competitive insights.
Why Join?

- Daily gameplay tips and tricks.

- Meta discussions on the best characters and builds.

- Fan theories and anime/manga lore connections to the game.

Pro Tip: Upvote guides and tier lists to help the community grow!

3. GAMEFAQS & IGN BOARDS

Best for: Detailed guides, hidden mechanics, and FAQs for newcomers.
Why Join?

- Long-form text guides with step-by-step mission walkthroughs.

- Archived discussions on older game mechanics and Easter eggs.

- Deep dive comparisons of combat strategies and character strengths.

Pro Tip: Use GameFAQs message boards to find hidden unlock methods for secret characters.

4. STEAM COMMUNITY & PLAYSTATION/XBOX FORUMS

Best for: Troubleshooting game issues, finding multiplayer teammates, and reading patch discussions.
Why Join?

- Direct interaction with developers for bug reports and feedback.

- Organize PvP tournaments and challenge rival players.

- Discuss trophy/achievement hunting strategies.

Pro Tip: Check the Steam Guides section for user-made walkthroughs!

Joining these forums and communities helps you:
Stay updated on the latest game patches and balance changes.
Find the best character builds for both PvE and PvP.
Connect with top-tier players and get exclusive gameplay tips.
Access hidden Easter eggs, unlockables, and community challenges.

Final Tip: Being active in these communities can also give you inside scoops on upcoming DLCs before they're officially announced!

10.2 DEVELOPER UPDATES AND PATCH NOTES

To stay ahead in competitive play, you need to be aware of patch notes, buffs, nerfs, and balance updates that can change the meta. Game developers frequently release updates to fix bugs, adjust character power levels, and add new content.

WHERE TO FIND THE LATEST PATCH NOTES & DEVELOPER UPDATES

OFFICIAL BLEACH: REBIRTH OF SOULS WEBSITE

Why Check Here?

- The first source for official patch notes and balance changes.

- DLC announcements and character additions get posted first.

- Technical fixes and quality-of-life improvements are listed here.

Pro Tip: Bookmark the Patch Notes section to stay informed.

TWITTER/X & OFFICIAL SOCIAL MEDIA PAGES

Why Check Here?

- Developers often post teasers for upcoming features before official announcements.

- Quick updates on server maintenance, bug fixes, and event schedules.

- Fan interactions sometimes influence future game changes.

Pro Tip: Follow the game's official Twitter/X for developer Q&As and live updates.

PATCH NOTES BREAKDOWN ON YOUTUBE & TWITCH

Why Check Here?

- Popular gaming YouTubers and streamers analyze patch changes in real time.

- Side-by-side gameplay comparisons show how buffs/nerfs affect characters.

- Developers sometimes reveal upcoming patches during live streams.

Pro Tip: Look for "Rebirth of Souls Patch Analysis" videos after every update.

Each patch update usually includes:

Balance Changes – Adjustments to character abilities, damage output, and cooldowns.
Bug Fixes – Fixing game-breaking glitches or unintended exploits.
New Features & DLCs – Additional characters, story content, and online events.
Event Updates – Limited-time PvP tournaments, special missions, and community challenges.

Final Tip: After a major patch, test your favorite characters in Training Mode to adjust your strategy!

10.3 DLC AND FUTURE EXPANSIONS

The *BLEACH: Rebirth of Souls* universe is constantly evolving, with new characters, story expansions, game modes, and balance updates keeping the experience fresh. DLC (Downloadable Content) and future expansions bring exciting new battles, transformations, and exclusive features that every dedicated player should look forward to.

UPCOMING DLC EXPANSIONS & WHAT TO EXPECT

DLC PACK 1: "THE THOUSAND-YEAR BLOOD WAR"

New Playable Characters: Yhwach, Uryu (Schrift Form), Squad Zero Members
New Story Missions: Experience the Soul Society's final stand against the Quincy invasion.
New Bankai Forms: Ichigo's True Bankai and Renji's So-oh Zabimaru will be added.

New PvP Arena: Fight in The Royal Palace, an iconic battleground from the anime.

Release Window: Expected soon after launch, following the anime's final episodes.

DLC PACK 2: "HELL ARC AWAKENING" (SPECULATED)

New Story Mode Expansion: Based on Tite Kubo's new "Hell Arc" manga chapter.
 Playable Characters: Hollowfied Captains, Ichigo's Hell Transformation, and Hell Guardians.
 Special Game Mode: A survival-style raid mode featuring endless waves of Hell Beasts.

Why This Matters: The Hell Arc is a mystery-filled, unexplored storyline, and this DLC might reveal secrets about fallen Soul Reapers and their fate in Hell.

SEASONAL DLCS & LIMITED-TIME EVENTS

Apart from major expansions, the developers are likely to release:

 Character Packs – Additional fan-favorite fighters like Fullbringer Ginjo or Aizen's Chair Form.
 Crossover Events – Special BLEACH x Jump crossover battles with characters from other Shonen franchises.
 Holiday-Themed Events – Expect Christmas, Halloween, and New Year-themed Zanpakuto skins and outfits.

Final Tip: If you're serious about *BLEACH: Rebirth of Souls*, consider buying the Season Pass to get all DLCs at a discount.

To avoid missing out on pre-orders, bonuses, and early access:

Follow the official website and social media pages for announcements.
Check the PlayStation/Xbox/PC storefronts for pre-order discounts.
Join community discussions where leaks and early gameplay insights
often surface.

Pro Tip: Many DLC characters and weapons come with early access
bonuses, so grab them as soon as they drop!

10.4 WHERE TO FIND MORE GUIDES AND TUTORIALS

Whether you need expert combat tips, in-depth character builds, or secret
unlockables, there are tons of resources available to sharpen your skills in
BLEACH: Rebirth of Souls.

BEST PLACES FOR PROFESSIONAL GAME GUIDES

1. OFFICIAL STRATEGY GUIDE (PHYSICAL & DIGITAL)

The official game guidebook offers developer-approved strategies, hidden
lore, and concept art.
Best for: 100% completionists, lore fans, and collectors.

Where to Buy: Available on Amazon, PlayStation/Xbox digital stores, and
major retailers.

2. YOUTUBE CONTENT CREATORS & STREAMERS

Popular gaming YouTubers and Twitch streamers provide real-time breakdowns of:

- Character tier lists & PvP rankings.

- Speedrun strategies & hidden game mechanics.

- Secret unlocks & glitch exploits (before patches nerf them!).

Top Channels to Watch: Search for "BLEACH: Rebirth of Souls Pro Tips" to find high-level gameplay.

3. GAMEFAQS & IGN WALKTHROUGHS

Detailed text-based guides covering every aspect of the game.
Best for: Players who prefer written explanations over video tutorials.

Where to Find Them: Just Google "Bleach Rebirth of Souls Walkthrough GameFAQs".

4. DISCORD COMMUNITIES & REDDIT FORUMS

The best place to find real-time discussions, tier list debates, and hidden Easter eggs.
Best for: Competitive players, speedrunners, and casual fans looking for PvE tips.

Final Tip: Being active in Discord & Reddit communities gives you access to the latest leaks and upcoming DLC news before they're officially announced!

www.ingramcontent.com/pod-product-compliance
Lightning Source LLC
Chambersburg PA
CBHW071004050326
40689CB00014B/3479